LOW-CARB CRAVINGS COOKBOOK

LOW-CARB
CRAVINGS
COOKBOOK

YOUR FAVORITE FOODS
Made Low-Carb

FOREWORD BY

Jennifer Koslo, PhD, RD

ROCKRIDGE
PRESS

CONTENTS

FOREWORD

Jennifer Koslo, PhD, RD
AUTHOR OF *DIABETIC COOKBOOK FOR TWO*

As a Registered Dietitian, I know that you can add years to your life by making a habit of eating well and exercising regularly. But there is no one-size-fits-all diet that works for everyone.

The majority of people struggling with weight issues are in need of guidance to help them make sustainable dietary and lifestyle changes amid the mixed messages and confusing advice constantly circulated in the media. For me, helping people achieve a healthy weight and enjoy a higher quality of life is a top priority.

How is it possible to achieve a healthy weight? Recent research points to diets that include nonstarchy vegetables, fruits, lean animal proteins, plant proteins, healthy fats (olive oil, nuts, avocados), and foods low in refined carbohydrates at each meal. And indeed many people are finding great initial success with low-carb diets when they strike the right healthy balance of these components. But what happens after the weight loss stalls or boredom sets in? A good number of folks falter, longing for their favorite higher-carb foods and treats.

Eliminating sugars and grains can be the biggest roadblock for maintaining a low-carb diet that lasts for the long term. Eating styles that are too restrictive can never be successful in the final analysis because they set the body up for cravings or, even worse, nutritional deficiencies. In order to make changes that are sustainable, there has to be moderation, variety, and balance.

The low-carb recipes offered in this book are designed to help you uncover the root cause of your cravings and satisfy them with flavorful recipes that tackle all of your sweet, salty, fatty, greasy, and chocolaty desires while helping you keep your total carb count in check. Your favorite high-carb recipes are given a makeover by replacing high-carb grains and flours with lower-carb healthy alternatives like almond and coconut flour. If you have been craving pasta, you'll be pleasantly surprised and deeply pleased by how clever cuts of vegetables are used to give you the same type of textures and flavors without the carbs. No matter what your preferences or dietary restrictions are, you'll find many recipes in this book to gratify you while allowing you to stay on track during your most vulnerable dieting moments.

The best way to satisfy a craving is to give in a little but to do so in moderation and to do it by eating good-tasting food made with nutritious ingredients. If you are committed to a low-carb lifestyle, then this book is for you.

INTRODUCTION

Pancakes, mashed potatoes, nachos, grilled cheese, pizza, cupcakes, chicken potpie . . . classic, comforting, and loaded with carbs! Isn't this book supposed to help you stick to your low-carb diet? Absolutely. If cheating on your diet is your dirty little secret, consider this book a big clean reward. All these favorite foods, and more, can still be yours and help satisfy those nagging cravings—but in a low-carb kind of way. All it takes is a few adjustments to key ingredients and cooking methods.

If you've been following a low-carb diet for a while now, you know exactly what saps your will to continue. It's those cravings, and feelings of deprivation, that arise after a while, once the monotony of your regular meals sets in. Acting on them can bring your diet crashing down around you. Stay strong and read on.

This cookbook does not attempt to offer recipes for low-carb living, day in and day out—surely you already have one or more cookbooks for your daily needs. Instead, this book will be your salvation for the weak moments, when the cravings hit. Don't believe it? Try any of these recipes:

> Good morning! BISCUITS AND GRAVY (PAGE 37) are back on the menu, thanks to coconut flour.

> Ready for a snack? CHICKEN FINGERS (PAGE 71) are in your future, with a crispy kick from almond flour.

> Piiiizzzzaaaaaa. Let's keep it hush-hush, but fans of MEAT LOVER'S PIZZA (PAGE 112) have the humble cauliflower to thank for bringing this beauty back.

> Missing a bowl full of noodles? Start twirling CHICKEN PAD THAI WITH PEANUT SAUCE (PAGE 131), which subs spaghetti squash for carb-heavy rice noodles.

> Don't skip dessert. Start spooning STRAWBERRY ICE CREAM (PAGE 153), a rich, creamy confection made low-carb by coconut milk.

These tweaks allow you to stay on plan while still enjoying the flavors and spirit of the high-carb foods you crave. Here's to treating but not cheating!

CHAPTER 1

A TASTE OF THE FORBIDDEN

On a low-carb eating plan, what once was the norm is now "forbidden"—and the forbidden always seems more desirable. Staying committed to any diet requires discipline, variety, and balance. The health benefits you'll achieve are a given, so finding ways to stay motivated and dedicated to your low-carb lifestyle is key to achieving success. This cookbook will give you that taste of the forbidden to help you manage cravings for high-carb indulgences while still honoring your plan.

Over the past few decades, numerous studies have shown how effective low-carb diets are for improving several health markers. For example, the April 2004 issue of *The Journal of Nutrition* contained a study demonstrating that very low-carb diets were effective at improving characteristics associated with metabolic syndrome, a combination of conditions—including increased blood pressure, high blood sugar, excess body fat at the waist, and abnormal cholesterol levels—that increase the risk of heart disease, stroke, and diabetes.

Another study, in the May 22, 2003, issue of *The New England Journal of Medicine*, compared low-carb diets to low-fat diets and concluded that weight loss, triglycerides, insulin sensitivity, and fasting blood glucose all improved most significantly on low-carb diets.

So, while these diets are highly effective, many find them difficult to follow for a long period due to their restrictive nature.

If you've eaten a low-fat, low-calorie diet all your life, sausage for breakfast, bacon for lunch, and steak for dinner may sound like a food vacation. But, eventually, even on the most exotic vacation, everyone gets homesick for the familiar . . . and that's when it hits: the craving for your high-carb favorites.

For many, these cravings grow so severe they become the reason to cheat and, possibly, even quit the diet altogether. Fortunately, cravings don't have to be your downfall. You can replace your favorite high-carb foods with lower-carb versions that keep you on plan and satisfied.

THE LOW-CARB COMMITMENT

Eating a low-carbohydrate diet requires personal commitment. At first it may seem easy because you've learned low-carb diets not only help you lose weight and get healthier but also leave you feeling very satiated. The food is tasty. The weight comes off quickly. You feel satisfied, rarely hungry, and motivated.

Then, one day, when everything seems to be going your way, a powerful craving for a favorite high-carb food hits, and your progress is threatened. Many people are surprised when high-carb cravings derail their diet. Be aware, and plan accordingly.

C-R-A-V-I-N-G, FIND OUT WHAT IT MEANS TO ME

Nearly everyone has food cravings of some sort. Cravings, which are different from the basic biological urge of hunger, tend to center on an intense desire for a specific food, like chocolate, or type of food, such as spicy. Cravings may occur in conjunction with hunger, or they may be entirely separate. Hungry or not, a food craving can be difficult to ignore.

Commonly, cravings are centered on specific tastes or textures. For example, people may crave sweet, sour, salty, bitter, or umami (the "fifth" taste—savory) foods. They may also crave something fatty, spicy, or crunchy.

The most common cravings tend to be for foods high in carbohydrates, which, perhaps not surprisingly, are also high in sugar. According to a Massachusetts Institute of Technology study, people and animals show "sugar-seeking" behaviors similar to the types of drug-seeking behaviors found in addicts. This powerful pull to sugar, and foods containing it in the form of refined carbohydrates, can cause all kinds of cravings.

While food cravings can vary from culture to culture, some foods from the Standard American Diet are craved most commonly in the West. These foods include:

> Baked goodies, like cookies
> Bread and pasta
> Caffeine-containing foods and beverages, such as coffee
> Candy
> Chocolate
> Fatty, salty foods, such as potato chips or French fries
> Fizzy drinks, like soda or energy drinks
> Greasy, meaty foods, like hamburgers
> Pizza
> Starchy comfort foods, like mac and cheese or mashed potatoes

This cookbook contains recipes for many of these most-craved foods. In fact, 8 of the 10 categories are covered. They include muffins, pastas, cookies and candy, pizzas, burgers and chili dogs, French fries, onion rings, chocolate, and starchy comfort foods like macaroni and cheese. These recipes will help you satisfy those temptations when they arise—and still maintain your health and diet goals.

Cravings: They're Not All in Your Head

Food is an integral part of culture, social engagement, and family life. Food has strong associations with memories, good times, and even love. There may be certain foods you've adored since childhood that are now out of reach because they are high in refined carbohydrates. These foods, strongly associated with comfort, tradition, and memories, may have an emotional pull that is difficult to resist.

Along with an emotional connection to food, there may be physical reasons for cravings, as well. If you've followed the Standard American Diet (SAD) most of your life, eating macronutrient ratios according to the USDA's food pyramid, then you've probably been eating a lot of refined carbohydrates. Foods high in refined carbohydrates can actually be addicting, according to a 2013 study from Boston Children's Hospital published in *Medscape Medical News*.

With that emotional connection, as well as a potential physical addiction to certain foods, it's understandable that cravings arise—even when you've made the choice to eliminate those foods from your life. The trick, then, becomes finding ways to manage these cravings while maintaining your healthy new lifestyle.

THE LOW-CARB LIFESTYLE

Choosing a low-carb lifestyle isn't a temporary solution to weight or health issues. Instead, it is a lifelong commitment to your health. Long-term success depends upon continued carbohydrate restriction. However, to realistically maintain the diet for a lifetime, you also need some sensible recipes that allow you to eat the foods you crave and still stay on plan.

Most diets provide tips and direction on how to succeed long-term and maintain weight loss and health gains. For example, the Atkins diet offers several phases that gradually ramp up healthy carb intake. By phase three and four, you move into pre-maintenance and maintenance phases, which allow you to make sensible choices for a lifetime of low-carbohydrate eating. Though you'll eat more carbs in these phases, you still won't be going hog-wild. You'll always need to restrict carbs on some level to maintain results.

By now, you probably have a host of recipes and meals that adhere to the plan's requirements. You know which foods fit your lifestyle and which are best avoided. Still, even with this knowledge and experience, cravings may lurk just around the corner.

Fortunately, there's no need to fall off the low-carb wagon to satisfy those cravings. You can give in a little by choosing modified versions of foods that

WHAT IS THE KETO DIET?

While most people have heard of the granddaddy of low-carb diets, the Atkins Diet, fewer people have heard of the Keto (or ketogenic) Diet. The popularity of the Keto Diet has surged in recent years, and many people are finding success on this low-carb, high-fat plan.

Atkins talks mostly about carb counts. On the Keto Diet, it is important to monitor fat, too. Fortunately for your palate, you monitor fat to ensure you are getting enough of it, not restricting it.

The goal of the Keto Diet is to enter *ketosis*, a state in which your body burns stored fat as fuel instead of glucose or carbohydrates. You do this by limiting carbs and increasing fat in order to control blood glucose so your body releases less insulin. Since both protein and carbohydrates cause blood glucose to rise and insulin to

spike, a ketogenic diet relies on fat consumption instead, which has the most negligible effect on blood glucose and insulin.

A typical ketogenic diet recommends eating at least 70 percent of your calories from fat, with about 25 percent of calories coming from protein and 5 percent from carbs. This can quickly kick your body into deep fat burning, which is perfect for weight loss.

If you're feeling stalled in your current plan and want to read a more in-depth

introduction to the Keto Diet, the authoritative book on the subject is *Keto Clarity: Your Definitive Guide to the Benefits of a Low-Carb, High-Fat Diet* by Jimmy Moore and Eric Westman, MD. An excellent companion cookbook to it is *Bacon & Butter: The Ultimate Ketogenic Diet Cookbook* by Celby Richoux, which offers 150 keto-friendly recipes.

are lower in carbs than their traditional counterparts. Of course, if you do eat these crave busters, the best way to balance this is to adjust carb counts throughout the rest of the day or week so carb levels stay close to those prescribed by your current eating plan and phase.

The recipes in this book remain very close to your low-carb plan allotments. While slightly higher in carbs than the typical low-carb foods you eat—some with as many as 5 grams of net carbs more than other foods—they aren't going to blow your entire carb budget. Instead of giving in to cravings with the "forbidden" versions of these foods, use these lower-carb versions to indulge, and adjust your remaining carb counts accordingly. Think of it as part of a winning strategy to maintain your healthy-living plan for the long term.

LOW-CARB RECIPES FOR HIGH-CARB CRAVINGS

This book contains 105 low-carb recipes to battle those high-carb cravings in nine different categories. They run the gamut from simple condiments like barbecue sauce (commercial varieties almost always contain sugar) to delicious desserts. You'll also find low-carb substitutes for pasta, pizza, tasty casseroles and noodle dishes, sandwiches, chilies, soups and stews, snacks, sides, and breakfasts.

Ingredient Substitutions

These recipes lower carbs drastically from their original versions by substituting ingredients with less starch and sugar. All eliminate high-carb processed ingredients like sugar, white flour, pasta, and rice. In their place, baked goods may call for almond or coconut flour to replace all-purpose flour. In addition to the carbohydrate savings per serving, this substitution also makes the recipes gluten-free. Likewise, sauces and stews may contain puréed vegetables to thicken them instead of a traditional high-carb flour roux, or they may be thickened with a low-carb cheese. Low-carb full-fat dairy replaces high-carb low-fat dairy products.

In baking, natural sweeteners like stevia, erythritol, and inulin replace sugar, adding sweetness without carbohydrates. The recipes are free of artificial sweeteners like aspartame and sucralose, which have been shown to spike blood sugar.

Specially cut vegetables replace pasta, rice, and starchy potatoes, giving you all the flavors and textures without the carbs. For sandwiches, you may make special bread using coconut or almond flour, you may use low-carb tortillas, or the sandwich may take another form, such as a lettuce wrap.

In some cases, you will find the flavor you love in your high-carb favorites, but the recipe may take a bit of creative license. For example, a favorite sandwich may have its craveable flavors translated into a tasty soup or stew.

Nutritional Information

Each recipe contains complete nutritional information per serving, including both total and net grams of carbohydrates, calories, protein, fat, fiber, and sodium. In some cases, the servings may be smaller than you're used to. This keeps the carb counts low but you'll get enough to satisfy your craving.

The main dish recipes contain fewer than 25 net grams of carbohydrates per serving, while snacks and desserts contain fewer than 20 net grams of carbs per serving. These carbohydrate levels should fit well within a maintenance-phase low-carb eating plan.

Ninety recipes are gluten-free. If you are gluten sensitive or have celiac disease, you can still consume many of your favorites, modified, without having to worry about the impact of gluten. All these changes allow you to eat some of your high-carb favorites in a tasty, low-carb form.

Portion Is Key

As previously mentioned, you may notice that some of the portions are smaller than you may be used to. To satisfy cravings and keep your diet low in carbs, portion control is essential. Chances are, at this point in your diet, you have the low-carb part down. When you first started the diet, you may have struggled with portion control. However, as your body switched to burning fat for fuel in place of burning glucose, you may have noticed that it became easier to control portions.

When you're satisfying a craving, however, portion control may be more difficult. When you're eating something you haven't tasted in a while, you're craving it, and it tastes really good, it can be difficult not to do a face plant and eat the entire dish. While one serving of any of these dishes meets the criteria for a low-carb diet, eating the entire dish in one sitting does not. It is essential that you stick to the recommended portion sizes and don't eat more than one serving in a day. You can share with family and friends, or freeze leftovers in single-portion sizes for those future cravings. If you're still hungry, fill the space with lower-carb fare, such as leafy greens.

Portion control is an essential part of maintaining all your losses and hard work on a low-carb diet. These recipes are all written with portion control in mind. They help you satisfy cravings while still keeping you on the low-carb track.

THE CRAVINGS KITCHEN

To satisfy your high-carb cravings with carb-friendly options, you'll need to keep your pantry appropriately stocked so you're ready when the craving hits. Pantry items are those you can keep in the freezer or on cupboard shelves and that don't need replacing often, or those you use frequently. Some of these are standard low-carb fare, while others may be different from items you've purchased in the past. If you have cravings for some types of food more frequently, you'll learn to stock your pantry accordingly.

The Pantry

Canned and Bottled Items

> BLACK SOYBEANS, CANNED: These are great when you want to use legumes because they are so low in carbs and very high in fiber. Half a cup of black soybeans contains 8 grams of carbs and 7 grams of fiber, leaving just 1 net gram of carbohydrates. Magic!

> BROTH, CANNED: Chicken, beef, and vegetable broths make great bases for soups and stews. Choose those without added sugar, and read the nutritional information for carb counts. Select unsalted broth so you can control the seasoning levels in your finished dishes.

> COCONUT MILK, CANNED: Coconut is the perfect low-carb food. Reduce the liquid, and it makes great whipped cream. In soups, it adds creaminess. In other foods, it can substitute for milk. Buy full-fat coconut milk, and double-check that there is no added sugar.

> PUMPKIN, CANNED: Pumpkin is a flavorful way to reduce carbs in many dishes. Buy unsweetened pumpkin purée, not pumpkin pie filling, which has added sugar.

> SALSA: Use as a tasty, low-carb snack or condiment. Buy a brand that does not have added sugar, beans, or corn.

> TOMATOES, CANNED: Add flavor, without a ton of carbs! Buy tomato products that do not have added sugar listed as an ingredient. Keep on hand tomato paste, tomato sauce, whole tomatoes, and crushed tomatoes.

THE CRAVING IS IN THE FLAVOR, NOT THE CARB

When you have a craving, what you are most often really craving is the flavor, not the carbs. For example, when a pregnant woman craves pickles, it is actually the sour-acidic taste of the vinegar being craved, not the pickle itself.

If you think about cravings in that way, you'll see why the recipes in this book are so perfect for satisfying those cravings. They cover sweet, salty, fatty, greasy, or chocolaty while still removing a large portion of the usual carbs.

Here's an example. Say you're craving a Philly Cheesesteak (page 98) with its fatty, salty, melty, cheesy flavors. Steak is low in carbs. So are peppers, onions, and cheese. These are all the flavors that make the sandwich so darn delicious. Then there's the bread, which is what makes the sandwich so high in carbohydrates. In the grand scheme of the sandwich, the bread doesn't add a lot of its own unique flavor. It merely serves as a vehicle for delivering the other delicious tastes.

To give this recipe a low-carb makeover, all you need to do is eliminate the bread. The question, then, is what to use as a vessel for all that salty, meaty, cheesy goodness. In this case, a hollowed-out green bell pepper is the perfect solution. Making the sandwich as a stuffed pepper offers all the flavors without the carbs, satisfying your craving in an acceptable low-carb format.

Likewise, imagine you're craving another favorite: Fettuccine Alfredo (page 117). In this dish, two things make it very high in carbs: the pasta and the flour used to make the roux that thickens the sauce. The recipe in this book cuts the carbs by using a combination of cheese and full-fat dairy products to make a smooth, creamy, flavorful Alfredo sauce and replacing the noodles with zucchini. When you taste it, you'll realize this: It was the flavor of the dish you were craving, not those strands of semolina flour known as pasta.

Frozen Foods

> BLUEBERRIES: Relatively low in net grams of carbs, they are great in breakfast foods such as pancakes or muffins. If possible, find wild organic blueberries, which have the best flavor.

Pantry Items

> ALMOND FLOUR: Use in baking and in place of bread crumbs in recipes. In many recipes it works perfectly well by itself, although in some you may need to cut it with a bit of coconut flour to lighten the end result.

> BAKER'S CHOCOLATE, UNSWEETENED: Use in baked goods, puddings, and more. When combined with stevia, it's delicious.

> BAKING POWDER AND BAKING SODA: Not only are these leavening agents helpful in making baked goods, they also give battered and fried foods a bit of volume. Because you use such a small amount, the carbs are negligible.

> COCOA POWDER, UNSWEETENED: Cocoa powder gives you a base for smoothies and desserts to help satisfy those chocolate cravings.

> COCONUT FLOUR: Great in muffins, pancakes, and other baked goods, it also makes a fantastic substitute for hot cereal. In baking, it is sometimes used to lighten almond flour so the end result isn't quite as heavy.

> COCONUT OIL: Coconut oil withstands really high temperatures, so it's great for frying and sautéing. It's also loaded with healthy fat. Choose extra-virgin coconut oil that is solid at room temperature.

> DRIED HERBS AND SPICES: You probably have a lot of these in your pantry already, and they are great for adding flavor. Some dried herbs and spices to always have on hand include:

- Black pepper and peppercorns
- Cayenne pepper
- Chili powder
- Cinnamon, ground
- Cloves, ground
- Cumin, ground
- Garlic powder
- Italian seasoning
- Nutmeg, ground
- Paprika
- Red pepper flakes
- Rosemary, dried
- Sea salt
- Tarragon, dried
- Thyme, dried

> **MUSHROOMS, DRIED:** Reconstituting dried mushrooms in broth gives them a deep, delicious umami (savory) taste that adds flavor to many dishes, such as Cream of Mushroom Soup (page 79). If you can find them, dried porcini mushrooms offer the best flavor. Otherwise, any dried mushrooms will do.

> **OLIVE OIL, EXTRA-VIRGIN:** Olive oil is a very healthy, tasty oil. It works well in dressings and vinaigrettes, as well as for sautéing and baking.

> **PEANUT BUTTER:** Peanut butter is a perfect food for satisfying cravings. Use it in a peanut sauce for savory dishes, or in baked goods. Choose a smooth peanut butter without added sugar.

> **STEVIA:** A great natural sweetener, stevia doesn't spike blood glucose or affect insulin. You can buy powdered stevia in individual packets or in larger quantities to be measured as you use it. In general, *1 teaspoon of stevia equals the sweetness added by 1 cup of sugar.* For baking, choose a stevia that measures cup for cup like sugar, such as Truvia (see page 26).

> **VINEGARS:** Add lots of flavor without a lot of carbs (except for balsamic vinegar, which is high in carbs). Keep a selection of tasty vinegars on hand, such as apple cider vinegar, red wine vinegar, and white vinegar, for use in recipes.

Other

> **LOW-CARB TORTILLAS:** For someone on a low-carb diet, low-carb tortillas are a great occasional indulgence—if you don't have a problem with wheat or gluten. For some people, low-carb tortillas cause a stall in weight loss or a slight gain. You'll need to monitor your progress when you eat them to determine whether they work for you. If you don't do well with low-carb tortillas, replace them with large leaves of lettuce, which make great wraps.

> **PORK RINDS:** When ground in a food processor or blender, pork rinds make a fantastic zero-carb bread crumb replacement. Choose plain pork rinds, without any added MSG.

> **WINE:** Dry, unfortified wines (think Syrah, Chardonnay, Cabernet Sauvignon, and Pinot Grigio) are low in residual sugar, making them low in carbs. They can add tremendous flavor to cooking while keeping carbs reasonably low.

THE SWEET CHOICE

Many of the dessert recipes call for some type of sweetener. Because baking requires precise amounts of specific ingredients in order to obtain the appropriate texture and density, it is important to find a low-carb sweetener that measures like sugar.

While many low-carbers turn to artificial sweeteners like sucralose (Splenda) and aspartame (NutraSweet), recent research from Washington University and Yale University suggests that these sweeteners may actually *contribute* to weight gain and increase sugar and carbohydrate cravings. Furthermore, these sweeteners are made from chemicals, and there is a great deal of controversy about their long-term effects on health. As such, these artificial sweeteners are not the ideal choice for low-carb baking.

One natural sweetener, stevia, seems to have fewer side effects than artificial sweeteners. An August 2010 study in the journal *Appetite* measured the effects of stevia, sucralose, and aspartame on hunger, satiety, blood glucose, and insulin secretion. Only the stevia showed lower post-meal glucose and insulin secretion, suggesting it has a negligible effect on blood sugar, making it an excellent choice for low-carb diets.

Other studies show that the sugar alcohol erythritol also has a negligible effect on blood glucose and insulin. Because erythritol measures more like sugar than stevia does, this makes it a good choice for low-carb baking as well.

A few different sweeteners may be ideal for the baking recipes in this cookbook because they measure like sugar while having negligible effects on blood glucose and insulin secretion.

> **TRUVIA BAKING BLEND:** Found in the baking section of most grocery stores, Truvia Baking Blend is a mixture of stevia and erythritol. It measures cup for cup like sugar. Select the baking blend, and not some other form of Truvia, or it won't measure correctly in the recipes.

> **SWERVE:** While Swerve can be a bit difficult to find locally (check local health food stores), it is widely available from online retailers such as Amazon.com. Swerve contains a blend of erythritol and inulin, a fiber derived from chicory. It has a negligible effect on blood glucose and insulin secretion and doesn't have any bitter aftertaste. It is available as confectioners' sugar and as granulated sugar. This sweetener also behaves much like sugar in cooking. For example, you can use it to make a simple syrup, or you can caramelize it.

> **STEVIA**: Powdered stevia is excellent for recipes that don't require precise measurements. For example, it is good in a pudding. It is less effective in baking unless combined with some type of bulking agent such as fruit juice, applesauce, or mashed bananas. However, combining stevia with a bulking agent adds more carbohydrates to the end result, making it less than ideal for low-carbohydrate baking. Stevia is very sweet. As noted previously, 1 teaspoon of stevia equals the sweetness of about 1 cup of sugar. Some people find its slightly bitter aftertaste unpleasant, while others don't notice it at all.

Note: In this book, recipes that require the sweetener to measure cup for cup like sugar list "sweetener" as the ingredient. Choose Truvia Baking Blend or Swerve for these recipes. Other recipes that need sweetness without bulk call for stevia, which comes in packets.

The Tools

If you're cooking low-carb already, chances are you have some great tools for preparing your meals. The kitchen tools listed here are quite helpful for preparing the recipes in this book. Consider adding some to your kitchen if you don't own them already.

> **BAKING PANS:** You will need at least one nonstick rimmed baking sheet, as well as a 9-inch square baking dish and a 9-by-13-inch baking pan. Other sizes, such as loaf pans, pie plates, and springform pans, are also helpful.

> **BLENDER:** While you can make smoothies in a food processor, a blender works better. There are many affordable options for this handy kitchen tool.

> **DUTCH OVEN:** This is perfect for cooking soups, stews, and other foods. Choose a sturdy Dutch oven with a lid that can go from stove top to oven.

> **FOOD PROCESSOR:** If you can afford one (and there are many affordable options), get a food processor. It is invaluable for chopping, shredding, blending, and mixing—all frequent activities in a low-carb kitchen.

> **JULIENNE PEELER, MANDOLINE, AND SPIRAL SLICER:** While this isn't absolutely necessary, a *julienne peeler* is a super-handy tool. It works like a vegetable peeler, but instead of giving you a long ribbon strip, it gives you thin noodles. It's a good alternative to the spiral slicer if you're on a budget. You can find very affordable *mandolines*, and they make perfect, thin slices. Choose one with a guard so you can be sure to julienne or slice the vegetables, not your fingers. The spiral slicer is a nifty kitchen tool perfect for turning veggies into pasta in a snap. If you're a pasta craver, this is the tool for you. Hand-crank spiral slicers, which are about $50, are the most versatile and do the best job. You can also purchase an hourglass spiral slicer, but you'll be limited to small, thin veggies like carrots and zucchini, and you won't be able to make as many cool noodle shapes.

> **SKILLETS:** You'll need a large (12-inch) skillet. Having one that is nonstick is helpful but not necessary. A cast iron skillet is a great choice because it goes from stove top to oven easily.

> **VEGETABLE PEELER:** Vegetable peelers are essential for peeling, but they also allow you to turn zucchini into wide lasagna noodles and to create ribbon-shaped "pasta" from other veggies.

FIVE TIPS FOR DEALING WITH CRAVINGS

1. **PAY ATTENTION TO HOW YOU FEEL EMOTIONALLY.** Sometimes cravings arise because of stress, anger, sadness, or other emotions (heck, sometimes people have cravings because they are in a celebratory mood). Instead of using food to stop the craving, allow yourself to experience the emotion and work through it.

2. **REEVALUATE YOUR EATING HABITS.** Make sure you are eating a wide variety of foods to meet your body's nutritional needs, and that you're eating enough food. Not eating enough, or getting insufficient nutrition, can trigger cravings.

3. **REMOVE YOURSELF FROM SITUATIONS THAT TRIGGER CRAVINGS.** Television ads are a perfect example of this. If you're suddenly craving something while watching television, step away and, if you're truly hungry, eat something low in carbs to get you over the hump.

4. **DRINK WATER.** Sometimes dehydration can trigger cravings. When you have a craving, drink a glass of water and wait 20 minutes to see if it passes.

5. **EAT PLENTY OF FAT.** Fat is very satisfying, and your body craves it. If you eat a diet with enough fat, it will satisfy you and help keep cravings at bay.

RECIPE GUIDE

While we may be united by our cravings for carbs, our dietary restrictions differentiate us. With this in mind, we've made a point of adding labels to the recipes so you know if they are compatible with your diet. Here's what you'll see:

GF for gluten-free

V for vegetarian

DF for dairy-free

Each recipe also notes the total prep time and cook time (if any) required to make it, so you can decide if the craving is worth the work. But just between us, it is.

CHAPTER 2

BREAKFASTS

BLUEBERRY MUFFINS

SERVES 6 ▪ PREP TIME: 10 MINUTES ▪ COOK TIME: 20 MINUTES, PLUS 10 MINUTES COOLING TIME

GF V

3 large eggs, beaten

¼ cup coconut milk

½ teaspoon vanilla extract

1¼ cups sweetener (Truvia Baking Blend or Swerve), divided into ¾ cup and ½ cup

⅛ teaspoon salt

⅓ cup coconut flour

¼ cup fresh blueberries

1 tablespoon ground cinnamon

4 tablespoons unsalted butter, melted

PER SERVING (1 muffin)
Calories: 201; Total carbs: 23g; Net carbs: 19g; Fiber: 4g; Fat: 13g; Protein: 5g; Sodium: 488mg

Blueberry muffins are delicious bundles of sweetness and sunshine. Unfortunately, standard blueberry muffins offer a ton of carbs. This recipe replaces the white flour with coconut flour and the sugar with a little bit of sweetener. Because these muffins are a breakfast treat, you probably won't want to eat them every day. However, they freeze well. Put them in a resealable plastic bag, and freeze for up to six months.

1 Preheat the oven to 350°F.

2 Line a 6-muffin tin with paper muffin liners.

3 In a large bowl, whisk together the eggs, coconut milk, vanilla, ¾ cup of sweetener, and the salt until well combined.

4 Stir in the coconut flour, stirring until just combined.

5 Carefully fold in the blueberries.

6 Spoon the batter evenly into the prepared muffin cups.

7 Bake for about 20 minutes, or until the tops are golden.

8 Remove from the oven and cool on a wire rack for 10 minutes.

9 In a small bowl, whisk together the remaining ¾ cup of sweetener and the cinnamon.

10 Dip the muffin tops into the melted butter and then into the cinnamon mixture.

11 Serve warm or cold.

WHY IT WORKS: What you're really craving is the flavor of the blueberries along with the sweetness of the muffin. The delicious blueberries and sweetened cinnamon topping fulfill those needs—with a fraction of the carbs.

PUMPKIN-SPICE MUFFINS

SERVES 6 ▪ PREP TIME: 10 MINUTES ▪ COOK TIME: 20 MINUTES, PLUS 10 MINUTES COOLING TIME

½ cup almond meal

⅓ cup coconut flour

¼ teaspoon baking soda

⅛ teaspoon salt

½ teaspoon ground cinnamon

¼ teaspoon ground cloves

¼ teaspoon ground ginger

½ cup sweetener (Truvia Baking Blend or Swerve)

1 large egg, beaten

1 teaspoon vanilla extract

1 cup pumpkin purée

PER SERVING (1 muffin)
Calories: 144; Total carbs: 25g;
Net carbs: 20g; Fiber: 5g; Fat: 6g;
Protein: 4g; Sodium: 117mg

Take a break or start your day with this tasty treat. Pumpkin is a fantastic low-carb ingredient, adding flavor, fiber, and lots of vitamins and minerals. These muffins are delightfully fragrant and deliciously tasty. They also freeze well. Save any leftovers in a resealable freezer bag so you can soothe your pumpkin craving at any time.

1 Preheat the oven to 350°F.

2 Line a 6-cup muffin tin with paper muffin liners.

3 In a medium bowl, whisk together the almond meal, coconut flour, baking soda, salt, cinnamon, cloves, and ginger.

4 In another medium bowl, whisk together the sweetener, egg, vanilla, and pumpkin until well combined.

5 Add the wet ingredients to the dry ingredients. Stir until just combined.

6 Spoon equal amounts of the batter into the cups of the prepared muffin tin.

7 Bake for about 20 minutes, or until a toothpick inserted in the center comes out clean.

8 Remove from the oven, cool on a wire rack for 10 minutes, and serve.

WHY IT WORKS: Almond meal by itself tends to make baked goods a bit heavy, while coconut flour alone tends to be extremely thirsty, requiring the addition of a significant amount of liquid. Combining the two helps diminish these properties, giving the muffins the right consistency. You'll have a moist, crumbly muffin to satisfy your craving.

BLUEBERRY PANCAKES

SERVES 4 ■ PREP TIME: 10 MINUTES ■ COOK TIME: 10 MINUTES

GF V

½ cup coconut flour

1 teaspoon baking powder

½ packet powdered stevia

¼ teaspoon salt

4 large eggs, beaten

1 cup coconut milk

½ teaspoon vanilla extract

1 cup fresh blueberries

2 tablespoons unsalted butter

PER SERVING (1 pancake)
Calories: 345; Total carbs: 19g;
Net carbs: 11g; Fiber: 8g; Fat: 27g;
Protein: 10g; Sodium: 249mg

There's just something about waking up to blueberry pancakes that gets your day off to a good start. These pancakes capture the essence of your favorite high-carb version while keeping carb counts in check using coconut flour and stevia. Since it's the pancakes you're craving, skip the syrup and instead top them with a pat of rich, creamy butter. You can substitute coconut oil for butter to make a dairy-free version.

1 In a large bowl, whisk together the coconut flour, baking powder, stevia, and salt.

2 In a medium bowl, whisk together the eggs, coconut milk, and vanilla.

3 Add the wet ingredients to the dry ingredients, stirring until just combined.

4 Carefully fold in the blueberries.

5 In a nonstick skillet over medium-high heat, melt the butter, swirling it to coat the pan.

6 Pour a scant ¼ cup of the batter into the heated pan for each pancake. Cook for about 5 minutes, or until bubbles form on the top.

7 Flip the pancakes. Continue cooking for about 5 minutes more, or until cooked through, and serve.

FRENCH TOAST

SERVES 2 ▪ PREP TIME: 10 MINUTES ▪ COOK TIME: 10 MINUTES

4 large eggs, beaten

¼ cup heavy (whipping) cream

1 teaspoon vanilla extract

Pinch salt

¼ teaspoon ground cinnamon

¼ teaspoon ground nutmeg

1 tablespoon unsalted butter

¼ teaspoon powdered stevia, divided

PER SERVING
Calories: 237; Total carbs: 2g;
Net carbs: 2g; Fiber: 0g; Fat: 20g;
Protein: 12g; Sodium: 248mg

Bonjour! For many people, French toast is breakfast perfection. With traditional French toast, the delicious vanilla custard soaks into bread, making a creamy yet hearty dish. This twist on French toast omits the bread altogether but still gives you the flavors you crave.

1 In a large bowl, whisk together the eggs, heavy cream, vanilla, salt, cinnamon, and nutmeg.

2 In a large nonstick skillet over medium-high heat, melt the butter.

3 Pour in the batter. Cook without stirring for about 5 minutes, or until firm.

4 Flip and cook the other side for 3 to 4 minutes more, or until firm.

5 Sprinkle with the stevia and serve.

WHY IT WORKS: How is this recipe different than scrambled eggs, and why does it taste like French toast? The trick is that you're essentially making the custard into which you would dip the bread to make it creamy and custardy. Here, you simply eliminate the middleman (the bread) and just cook the custard. Voilà—French toast flavor without all the carbs!

HASH BROWNS

SERVES 2 ▪ PREP TIME: 10 MINUTES, PLUS 20 MINUTES TO DRAIN ▪ COOK TIME: 15 MINUTES

GF V

2 yellow summer squash,
   such as pattypan,
   peeled and grated
1 tablespoon plus ½ teaspoon
   salt, divided
1 large egg, whisked
2 tablespoons unsalted butter

PER SERVING
Calories: 205; Total carbs: 16g;
Net carbs: 11g; Fiber: 5g; Fat: 15g;
Protein: 6g; Sodium: 1,547mg

Crispy, golden, and buttery on the outside and soft and fluffy on the inside, hash browns are the quintessential craveable breakfast food. Sadly, starchy potatoes are super high in carbs. While some people substitute sweet potatoes, their carb count remains fairly high as well. This recipe uses low-carb summer squash with an egg binder. The result gives you the buttery golden outside and the soft inside you crave. Breakfast is served.

1 In a colander set over the sink or a bowl, sprinkle the grated squash with 1 tablespoon of salt. Let sit for 20 minutes to allow the salt to draw out the water.

2 Quickly rinse the squash and pat dry with paper towels. Transfer it to a large bowl.

3 Add the whisked egg and remaining ½ teaspoon of salt. Mix well to combine.

4 In a medium nonstick skillet over medium-high heat, melt the butter.

5 Add the squash to the skillet. Cook for 5 to 7 minutes, without moving it, until golden brown.

6 Flip and cook the other side for 5 to 7 minutes more, until brown.

7 Cut in half and serve.

WHY IT WORKS: Drawing the water out of the squash with salt allows it to brown better, providing the desired golden texture. Meanwhile, this squash does give you great potato flavor when cooked, so it mimics hash browns with fewer carbs.

HAM AND SWISS QUICHE

SERVES 6 ▪ PREP TIME: 10 MINUTES ▪ COOK TIME: 30 MINUTES, PLUS 10 MINUTES COOLING TIME

GF

1½ tablespoons unsalted butter, divided

1½ tablespoons almond meal

½ onion, chopped

6 ounces cooked ham, diced

8 ounces Swiss cheese, grated

4 large eggs

1½ cups heavy (whipping) cream

½ cup water

½ teaspoon salt

¼ teaspoon freshly ground black pepper

PER SERVING (1 wedge)
Calories: 483; Total carbs: 5g; Net carbs: 4g; Fiber: 1g; Fat: 43g; Protein: 20g; Sodium: 799mg

Savory and satisfying, a ham and Swiss quiche starts your day in a hearty way. This recipe is for a fairly traditional quiche with one easy, carb-saving adjustment—eliminating the crust. By doing so, you not only make the quiche gluten-free, but you also cut out the biggest source of carbs.

1 Adjust the oven rack to the center of the oven.

2 Preheat the oven to 425°F.

3 With 1 tablespoon of butter, grease a 10-inch pie pan.

4 Sprinkle the pan with the almond meal.

5 In a large skillet over medium-high heat, heat the remaining ½ tablespoon of butter.

6 Add the onion and ham. Cook for about 5 minutes, stirring occasionally, until the onion is soft.

7 Transfer the onion and ham mixture to the prepared pie pan, spreading it evenly over the bottom.

8 Cover with the Swiss cheese.

9 In a medium bowl, whisk together the eggs, heavy cream, water, salt, and pepper.

10 Carefully pour the egg mixture over the onions, ham, and cheese.

11 Bake for about 25 minutes, or until the top is golden and the custard is set in the center.

12 Remove from the oven and cool for 10 minutes.

13 Cut into 6 wedges and serve.

DENVER OMELET

SERVES 2 ▪ PREP TIME: 10 MINUTES ▪ COOK TIME: 15 MINUTES

GF

4 large eggs, beaten

2 tablespoons heavy (whipping) cream

½ teaspoon salt

⅛ teaspoon freshly ground black pepper

2 tablespoons unsalted butter

3 scallions, chopped

½ green bell pepper, stemmed, seeded, and diced

4 ounces cooked ham, diced

4 ounces Cheddar cheese, grated

PER SERVING
Calories: 613; Total carbs: 7g; Net carbs: 5g; Fiber: 2g; Fat: 50g; Protein: 36g; Sodium: 1,888mg

With its savory ham, onions, green peppers, and cheese, the Denver omelet (sometimes called a southwestern omelet) is a very popular choice in diners across the country. This omelet is low enough in carbs that you can serve it with a side of the Hash Browns (page 34) and still stay below your carb count for the day. It's a great way to indulge your craving for a tasty diner-style breakfast.

1 In a medium bowl, whisk together the eggs, heavy cream, salt, and pepper until well combined. Set aside.

2 In a large nonstick skillet over medium-high heat, heat the butter until it shimmers.

3 Add the scallions, green bell pepper, and ham. Cook for about 5 minutes, stirring occasionally, until the vegetables are soft.

4 Transfer the ham and vegetables to a clean bowl and set aside.

5 Return the skillet to medium-high heat. Pour in the egg mixture. Cook for about 5 minutes, without touching it, until it begins to set around the edges.

6 Using a rubber spatula, carefully push the set edges away from the sides of the skillet toward the center. Tilt the skillet so any uncooked egg runs into the spaces around the edges. Continue cooking for about 3 minutes more, or until the new edges set.

7 Sprinkle the Cheddar cheese evenly over the omelet. Top half of the omelet with the reserved ham and vegetables. Cook for 2 to 3 minutes, or until the cheese begins to melt.

8 Fold the side of the omelet without the ham and vegetables over the other side. Tilt the pan over a large platter, and slide the omelet onto it.

9 Cut the omelet in half and serve.

BISCUITS AND GRAVY

SERVES 4 ▪ PREP TIME: 20 MINUTES ▪ COOK TIME: 35 MINUTES

`GF`

FOR THE BISCUITS

4 tablespoons unsalted butter, melted and cooled slightly

4 large eggs

½ teaspoon salt

½ teaspoon garlic powder

⅓ cup coconut flour

¼ teaspoon baking powder

FOR THE GRAVY

1 pound pork breakfast sausage

½ onion, diced

1 tablespoon coconut flour

½ cup unsalted chicken broth

1½ cups heavy (whipping) cream

½ teaspoon garlic powder

½ teaspoon dried sage

½ teaspoon salt

¼ teaspoon freshly ground black pepper

PER SERVING (2 biscuit halves and one-quarter of the gravy) Calories: 661; Total carbs: 11g; Net carbs: 7g; Fiber: 4g; Fat: 58g; Protein: 28g; Sodium: 1,791mg

Another popular and utterly craveable diner-style breakfast is this southern favorite—biscuits with sausage gravy. This breakfast is equal parts creamy, savory, flavorful, and satisfying, making it the perfect breakfast for those days when nothing else will do.

TO MAKE THE BISCUITS

1 Preheat the oven to 400°F.

2 Line a baking sheet with parchment paper.

3 In a large bowl, whisk together the butter, eggs, salt, and garlic powder.

4 Sift the coconut flour and baking powder into the eggs. Whisk until well combined.

5 Using a large spoon, drop the batter onto the prepared baking sheet in 4 equal amounts.

6 Bake for about 15 minutes, or until lightly browned.

7 Remove from the oven and cool for 10 minutes.

TO MAKE THE GRAVY

1 In a large skillet over medium-high heat, cook the breakfast sausage for about 5 minutes, or until browned, crumbling with a spoon.

2 Add the onion. Cook for about 4 minutes more, or until soft.

3 With a slotted spoon, transfer the sausage and onion to a platter. Reserve the rendered fat in the skillet.

4 Add the coconut flour to the rendered fat. Cook for 1 minute, stirring constantly.

5 Add the chicken broth. Cook for 1 to 2 minutes, stirring constantly, until thickened. ▸▸

6 Stir in the heavy cream, garlic powder, sage, salt, and pepper.

7 Cook for 3 to 4 minutes, stirring constantly, until the mixture is warmed through and thick.

8 Return the sausage and onion to the gravy, along with any juices that have collected on the platter. Cook for about 2 minutes more, stirring constantly, or until the sausage is heated.

9 Halve the biscuits, top with equal amounts of gravy, and serve.

TIMESAVING TIP: To save time, make the biscuits from a low-carb mix. There are many commercial low-carb biscuit mixes available, such as Carbquik Biscuit and Baking Mix and Bob's Red Mill Low-Carb Baking Mix. Find them on websites like Amazon.com and Netrition.com.

BREAKFAST STRATA

SERVES 8 ▪ PREP TIME: 20 MINUTES ▪ COOK TIME: 60 MINUTES

GF

Cooking spray

1 pound pork breakfast sausage

1 onion, diced

2 cups baby spinach

12 large eggs, beaten

½ cup heavy (whipping) cream

1 teaspoon salt

½ teaspoon freshly ground
    black pepper

1 teaspoon garlic powder

2 tablespoons Dijon mustard

8 ounces Cheddar cheese, grated

PER SERVING (1 square)
Calories: 412; Total carbs: 4g;
Net carbs: 2g; Fiber: 2g; Fat: 33;
Protein: 25g; Sodium: 1,082mg

Let's face it—sometimes you just crave brunch. Strata is a mainstay at brunches everywhere. The casserole, a savory, satisfying combination of eggs, bread, meat, and cheese, is delicious. This substitute for breakfast strata has all the same flavors and texture but without the whopping amount of carbs found in a traditional version.

1 Preheat the oven to 350°F.

2 Coat a 9-inch square pan with cooking spray.

3 In a large skillet over medium-high heat, cook the sausage for about 5 minutes, crumbling with a spoon, until browned.

4 Add the onion. Cook for 4 to 5 minutes more, stirring occasionally, until soft. Add the spinach and cook, continuing to stir occasionally for 2 more minutes. Remove the skillet from the heat and allow to cool slightly.

5 In a large bowl, whisk together the eggs, heavy cream, salt, pepper, garlic powder, and Dijon mustard until well combined.

6 Stir in the sausage and onion mixture, then fold in the Cheddar cheese.

7 Pour the mixture into the prepared pan. Bake for about 30 minutes, or until the eggs set and the cheese melts.

8 Remove from the oven and cool slightly.

9 Cut into 4 squares and serve.

TIMESAVING TIP: This recipe freezes well. If you crave foods like this often, double the recipe and freeze single-serving portions in resealable freezer bags so you'll be prepared when the next craving hits.

EGGS BENEDICT

SERVES 4 ▪ PREP TIME: 20 MINUTES ▪ COOK TIME: 35 MINUTES

GF

FOR THE ENGLISH MUFFINS
Cooking spray
¼ cup pork rinds, finely ground
¼ cup grated Asiago cheese
1 teaspoon baking powder
¼ teaspoon garlic powder
1 large egg, beaten
1 tablespoon sour cream
1 teaspoon white vinegar

FOR THE BACON, EGGS, AND HOLLANDAISE SAUCE
4 (1-ounce) slices Canadian bacon
1 tablespoon white vinegar
4 large eggs
2 egg yolks
½ teaspoon Dijon mustard
2 tablespoons freshly squeezed
   lemon juice
Pinch salt
4 tablespoons unsalted butter,
   melted and slightly cooled
   but still liquid

PER SERVING
Calories: 940; Total carbs: 4g;
Net carbs: 3g; Fiber: 1g; Fat: 72g;
Protein: 71g; Sodium: 2,774mg

Brunch lovers rejoice! Eggs Benedict is not out of your low-carb reach. The greatest number of carbs in this dish comes from the English muffins. Fortunately, you can eliminate them altogether, or, as this recipe does, replace them with a tasty low-carb alternative.

TO MAKE THE ENGLISH MUFFINS

1 Preheat the oven to 350°F.

2 Grease two 4-ounce ramekins with cooking spray.

3 In a large bowl, mix together the pork rinds, Asiago cheese, baking powder, garlic powder, egg, sour cream, and vinegar until well combined.

4 Evenly divide the mixture between the prepared ramekins.

5 Bake for 10 to 15 minutes, or until set and starting to brown.

6 Remove from the oven and place on a wire rack to cool.

7 Once cooled, remove the muffins from the ramekins and split each down the middle lengthwise.

8 Toast until browned.

TO MAKE THE BACON, EGGS, AND HOLLANDAISE SAUCE

1 In a large skillet over medium-high heat, cook the Canadian bacon for 2 to 3 minutes, or until warm and slightly crisp. Place 1 slice atop each muffin half.

2 Fill a large saucepan halfway with water. Add the vinegar. Place it over medium heat and bring to a simmer.

3 One at a time, carefully crack the whole eggs into the simmering water. Poach for about 5 minutes, or until set.

4 Using a slotted spoon, remove the eggs from the water. Blot them on paper towels. Place 1 egg atop each piece of Canadian bacon.

5 In a small glass bowl, whisk together the egg yolks, Dijon mustard, lemon juice, and salt.

6 Fill a medium saucepan halfway with water. Place it over medium heat and bring to a simmer. You can reuse the pan and water in which you poached the eggs if you wish, if your bowl is large enough to rest on its rim.

7 Set the bowl in the saucepan, with the bottom of the bowl just above the top of the simmering water. The bowl should not touch the water; empty some water if needed. Pour in the egg yolk mixture and whisk for about 5 minutes, or until it begins to thicken.

8 In a very thin stream, pour the melted butter into the yolk mixture, whisking constantly for about 3 minutes, or until the mixture is thick.

9 Spoon equal amounts of the sauce over each of the eggs and serve immediately.

TIMESAVING TIP: For an easier version of hollandaise sauce, make it in the microwave. In a microwave-safe bowl, whisk together the egg yolks, lemon juice, Dijon mustard, and salt. Then, in a thin stream, slowly whisk in the melted butter until incorporated. Microwave for 15 to 20 seconds on high to thicken. Whisk again before pouring it over the eggs.

SIDES

FRIED RICE

SERVES 4 ▪ PREP TIME: 10 MINUTES, PLUS 20 MINUTES TO DRAIN ▪ COOK TIME: 15 MINUTES

3 medium zucchini, sliced

1 tablespoon salt

3 tablespoons coconut oil

4 scallions, sliced

1 carrot, diced

4 ounces shiitake
    mushrooms, sliced

4 ounces cooked ham, diced

¼ teaspoon freshly grated ginger

3 garlic cloves, minced

2 large eggs, beaten

2 tablespoons soy sauce

½ teaspoon sesame oil

¼ teaspoon sriracha (optional)

PER SERVING
Calories: 229; Total carbs: 14g;
Net carbs: 10g; Fiber: 4g; Fat: 16g;
Protein: 11g; Sodium: 1,531mg

If you're one of the millions who crave Chinese food, then this recipe is for you! With classic Asian flavors, this fried rice hits the spot. Rest easy, though: This version contains far fewer carbs than the traditional dish. You won't miss Chinese takeout if you add this recipe to your arsenal.

1 In a colander placed over a bowl or the sink, sprinkle the zucchini slices with the salt. Let sit for 20 minutes so the salt can draw out the water.

2 Using a paper towel, wipe the salt off the zucchini and pat them dry.

3 Transfer the zucchini to a food processor fitted with a chopping blade. Pulse quickly 10 to 20 times, or until the zucchini resembles rice. Set aside.

4 In a large skillet over medium-high heat, heat the coconut oil until it shimmers.

5 Add the scallions, carrot, mushrooms, ham, and ginger. Cook for 5 to 7 minutes, stirring occasionally, until the vegetables are soft and begin to brown.

6 Add the garlic. Cook for about 30 to 60 seconds, stirring constantly, until fragrant.

7 Add the eggs. Cook for about 3 minutes more, stirring constantly, or until set.

8 Add the reserved zucchini, soy sauce, sesame oil, and sriracha (if using). Cook for about 4 minutes more, stirring occasionally, until the zucchini softens.

9 Serve.

WHY IT WORKS: Rice has a high starch content, making it high in carbohydrates. However, it really doesn't add a lot of flavor to the dish. Using a neutral-flavored, low-starch vegetable like zucchini bulks up the dish like rice would, without affecting the flavor. Zucchini, however, saves you a lot of carbs per serving, making it a great rice replacement.

MASHED POTATOES

SERVES 4 ▪ PREP TIME: 5 MINUTES ▪ COOK TIME: 15 MINUTES

GF V

1 head cauliflower, separated
    into florets

4 tablespoons unsalted
    butter, melted

¼ cup heavy (whipping) cream

½ teaspoon salt

¼ teaspoon freshly ground
    black pepper

PER SERVING
Calories: 144; Total carbs: 4g;
Net carbs: 2g; Fiber: 2g; Fat: 14g;
Protein: 2g; Sodium: 395mg

For many, mashed potatoes is the ultimate comfort food. That's why so many have difficulty giving up the starchy, buttery goodness when they go low carb. Mashed potatoes makes the perfect side for many dishes, including Chicken Fingers (page 71), steak, and many others. Take comfort in knowing that this version has the delicious flavors and textures you want, without all the carbs.

1 In a large pot over high heat, cover the cauliflower with water. Bring to a boil. Reduce the heat to medium. Simmer for 10 to 15 minutes, or until soft.

2 Drain the cauliflower.

3 Using a potato masher, blender, or food processor, mash the cauliflower until smooth.

4 To a large bowl, add the cauliflower, butter, heavy cream, salt, and pepper. Mix to combine, and serve.

WHY IT WORKS: When puréed, cauliflower takes on the texture of mashed potatoes. The butter and cream coat the cauliflower, giving it a luxurious mouthfeel that is consistent with mashed potatoes, with far fewer carbs.

RICE PILAF

SERVES 4 ⬝ PREP TIME: 5 MINUTES ⬝ COOK TIME: 15 MINUTES

GF V DF

1 head cauliflower, separated
　　into florets

2 tablespoons coconut oil

½ onion, diced

2 garlic cloves, minced

¼ cup pine nuts

½ teaspoon ground cumin

½ teaspoon ground cinnamon

½ teaspoon salt

¼ teaspoon freshly ground
　　black pepper

PER SERVING
Calories: 142; Total carbs: 7g;
Net carbs: 4g; Fiber: 3g; Fat: 13g;
Protein: 3g; Sodium: 312mg

Sometimes, rice pilaf is the only side dish that will satisfy. Some foods, like fish or chicken, seem made to go with this dish. In a traditional version, starchy rice provides a neutral, yet bulky, base that mixes well with pine nuts and dried fruits, creating a sweet and savory dish. Here, cauliflower substitutes, yielding a delicious, yet carb-friendly, alternative.

1 In a food processor fitted with a chopping blade, quickly pulse the cauliflower 10 to 20 times, or until it resembles rice. Set aside.

2 In a large skillet over medium-high heat, heat the coconut oil.

3 Add the onion. Cook for about 5 minutes, stirring occasionally, until soft.

4 Add the garlic. Cook for 30 to 60 seconds, stirring constantly, until fragrant.

5 Add the reserved cauliflower, pine nuts, cumin, cinnamon, salt, and pepper. Cook for about 6 minutes more, stirring frequently, until the cauliflower is heated through, and serve.

WHY IT WORKS: The dried fruit in traditional rice pilaf adds sweetness, but also carbs. Here, the cinnamon adds nearly carb-free sweetness, giving the dish a similar flavor but without the high-carb fruit.

PASTA SALAD

SERVES 4 ▪ PREP TIME: 20 MINUTES

GF V

FOR THE SALAD

3 medium zucchini, unpeeled and cut into ribbons with a vegetable peeler or mandoline

4 ounces cherry tomatoes, halved

½ red onion, very thinly sliced

10 fresh whole basil leaves, torn into small pieces

6 ounces mozzarella cheese, diced

1 (14-ounce) jar or can water-packed artichoke hearts, drained

½ red bell pepper, stemmed, seeded, and diced

FOR THE VINAIGRETTE

½ cup extra-virgin olive oil

2 tablespoons red wine vinegar

2 garlic cloves, minced

1 teaspoon Dijon mustard

1 teaspoon dried oregano

½ teaspoon salt

¼ teaspoon freshly ground black pepper

PER SERVING
Calories: 405; Total carbs: 15g; Net carbs: 11g; Fiber: 4g; Fat: 33g; Protein: 15g; Sodium: 836mg

Nothing says summer picnics like a delicious pasta salad. Sadly, pasta comes loaded with carbs. With almost no flavor of its own, the pasta provides filler and a neutral base that soaks up the tastes of the other ingredients. To cut the carbs, this salad uses zucchini instead—a neutral-flavored vegetable that blends beautifully with the other fresh, flavorful ingredients.

TO MAKE THE SALAD

1 Cut the zucchini ribbons in half crosswise, and put them in a large bowl.

2 Add the cherry tomatoes, red onion, basil, mozzarella cheese, artichoke hearts, and red bell pepper. Toss to combine.

TO MAKE THE VINAIGRETTE

1 In a small bowl, whisk together the olive oil, red wine vinegar, garlic, Dijon mustard, oregano, salt, and pepper.

2 Pour over the salad. Toss to combine, and serve.

TIMESAVING TIP: Many people find peeling and mincing garlic time consuming (and it makes your hands smell like garlic). A garlic press can save you! Put the whole unpeeled garlic clove in the press, and push it through over the bowl of vinaigrette. Then, remove the peel, add the next garlic clove, and repeat.

POTATO SALAD

SERVES 4 ▪ PREP TIME: 10 MINUTES ▪ COOK TIME: 15 MINUTES, PLUS 1 HOUR CHILLING TIME

`GF` `V`

- 1 head cauliflower, separated into florets
- 1 cup diced red onion
- 2 celery stalks, diced
- 6 large hardboiled eggs, chopped
- 2 dill pickle spears, diced
- 3 tablespoons chopped fresh chives
- 3 tablespoons chopped fresh parsley
- ½ cup mayonnaise
- ½ cup sour cream
- 2 tablespoons Dijon mustard
- 1 teaspoon salt
- ½ teaspoon freshly ground black pepper

PER SERVING
Calories: 311; Total carbs: 16g;
Net carbs: 13g; Fiber: 3g; Fat: 23g;
Protein: 12g; Sodium: 266mg

Summer barbecues and potlucks demand potato salad. It's the quintessential side dish with Bacon Cheeseburgers (page 102), Oven-Fried Chicken (page 136), and ribs. The potato provides a neutral flavor base for all the tasty ingredients in it—and the carbs. Here, cauliflower stands in. So, don't stay home. Take this dish, and you won't miss the carbs, or the picnic fun.

1 In a large pot over high heat, cover the cauliflower florets with water. Bring to a boil. Reduce the heat to medium. Simmer the cauliflower for 10 to 15 minutes, or until soft. Drain. Cool completely.

2 In a large bowl, stir together the cooled cauliflower, onion, celery, eggs, pickles, chives, and parsley. Mix well.

3 In a small bowl, whisk together the mayonnaise, sour cream, Dijon mustard, salt, and pepper.

4 Add the dressing to the cauliflower mixture. Toss well to combine.

5 Chill for 1 hour before serving.

CORN BREAD MUFFINS

SERVES 6 ▪ PREP TIME: 5 MINUTES ▪ COOK TIME: 15 MINUTES, PLUS 10 MINUTES COOLING TIME

Cooking spray

1 cup almond flour

1 teaspoon baking powder

¼ teaspoon salt

¼ teaspoon stevia

2 large eggs, beaten

3 tablespoons heavy (whipping) cream

1 tablespoon water

4 tablespoons unsalted butter, melted

PER SERVING
Calories: 139; Total carbs: 1g; Net carbs: 0.5g; Fiber: 0.5g; Fat: 14g; Protein: 3g; Sodium: 176mg

Nothing goes better with a heaping bowl of Chili Con Carne (page 81) than crumbly, sweet corn bread. Corn is very high in sugar, however, and corn bread typically contains honey. This means enough carbs to derail your low-carb diet. This recipe solves that, so dig in and enjoy.

1 Preheat the oven to 350°F.

2 Grease a 6-muffin tin with cooking spray. Set aside.

3 In a large bowl, sift together the almond flour, baking powder, salt, and stevia.

4 In a medium bowl, whisk together the eggs, heavy cream, water, and melted butter.

5 Add the wet egg mixture to the dry ingredients. Stir to combine.

6 Spoon equal amounts of the batter into the prepared muffin cups.

7 Bake for about 15 minutes, or until a toothpick inserted in the center comes out clean.

8 Remove from the oven and cool for 10 minutes.

9 Remove the muffins from the tin and serve.

WHY IT WORKS: The almond flour has a texture that is similar to cornmeal, giving the muffins the perfect crumbly texture. The stevia adds just enough sweet taste to mimic the honey in traditional corn bread.

POTATO SKINS

SERVES 2 ■ PREP TIME: 5 MINUTES ■ COOK TIME: 10 MINUTES, PLUS 10 MINUTES COOLING TIME

`GF`

Cooking spray

¾ cup grated Cheddar cheese, divided

4 bacon slices, cooked until crisp and crumbled, divided

½ cup sour cream, divided

6 scallions, sliced

PER SERVING
Calories: 544; Total carbs: 7g;
Net carbs: 6g; Fiber: 1g; Fat: 45g;
Protein: 28g; Sodium: 840mg

You *can* have perfect pub food at home—those delicious, perfectly crispy fried potatoes that are crunchy on the outside and soft on the inside. With traditional potato skins, the potatoes—which contain the bulk of the carbs—really take a back seat to the toppings. The true flavor comes from the bacon, sour cream, and crunchy scallions. This recipe has all of the flavors—minus the potatoes. They're pub-tastic!

1 Preheat the oven to 375°F.

2 Line a baking sheet with parchment paper. Coat with cooking spray.

3 Divide the cheese into 6 equal amounts. Pile them, a few inches apart, on the prepared sheet.

4 Evenly divide the crumbled bacon over the cheese piles.

5 Bake for about 10 minutes, or until the cheese is crisp and golden around the edges.

6 Remove from the oven and cool for about 10 minutes, or until hard and crispy.

7 Peel the hardened cheese crisps away from the parchment, and put them on a platter.

8 Top each crisp with 1 tablespoon of sour cream, and sprinkle with the scallions.

9 Serve immediately.

TIMESAVING TIP: You can also make the cheese crisps in the microwave. Line the microwave's turntable with parchment paper. Working in batches, spread the cheese into small circles on the parchment. Microwave for 30 to 40 seconds on high, until the cheese browns on the edges. Allow to cool slightly before peeling the crisps away from the paper. Top with the cooked bacon, sour cream, and scallions, and serve.

GREEN BEAN CASSEROLE

SERVES 4 ▪ PREP TIME: 15 MINUTES ▪ COOK TIME: 45 MINUTES

GF

FOR THE ONION STRAWS

¼ cup almond flour

¼ teaspoon garlic powder

½ teaspoon salt

⅛ teaspoon freshly ground
   black pepper

½ onion, very thinly sliced

2 large eggs, beaten

FOR THE CASSEROLE

1 pound green beans, trimmed

2 tablespoons unsalted butter

½ onion, thinly sliced

8 ounces mushrooms, sliced

½ cup unsalted chicken broth

¼ teaspoon garlic powder

1 teaspoon dried thyme

1 teaspoon salt

⅛ teaspoon freshly ground
   black pepper

½ cup sour cream

PER SERVING
Calories: 218; Total carbs: 15g;
Net carbs: 10g; Fiber: 5g; Fat: 15g;
Protein: 9g; Sodium: 1,066mg

What's a holiday without green bean casserole? This family favorite is rich and creamy, with savory flavors of mushrooms and crispy onions on top. With a few tweaks, it's easy to make this low-carb green bean casserole a part of any holiday table.

TO MAKE THE ONION STRAWS

1 Preheat the oven to 350°F.

2 Line a baking sheet with parchment paper.

3 In a medium bowl, whisk together the almond flour, garlic powder, salt, and pepper. Set aside.

4 In a small bowl, toss together the onions and beaten eggs. Remove the onions, allowing any excess egg to drip off.

5 Add the egg-coated onions to the almond flour mixture, and toss to coat.

6 Spread the coated onions in a single layer on the prepared sheet.

7 Bake for about 15 minutes, or until browned and crisp.

TO MAKE THE CASSEROLE

1 Place a large pot filled with water over high heat, and bring to a boil.

2 Add the green beans. Cook for about 5 minutes, or until crisp-tender.

3 Drain the green beans. Run cold water over them to stop the cooking. Allow any excess water to drain off, and transfer them to a large bowl.

4 In a large skillet over medium-high heat, heat the butter.

5 Add the onion and mushrooms. Cook for about 5 minutes, stirring occasionally, until soft.

6 Add the chicken broth, garlic powder, thyme, salt, and pepper. Cook for about 3 minutes, stirring occasionally, until the liquid evaporates.

7 Add the mixture to the bowl with the green beans. Stir to combine.

8 Stir in the sour cream.

9 Pour the green beans and sauce into a 9-inch pie pan. Bake for about 15 minutes, or until bubbly.

10 Remove from the oven. Top the casserole with the onion straws and serve.

TIMESAVING TIP: Use canned or frozen green beans, which have already been parboiled, to save time. Bake the onion straws and casserole on different racks at the same time to cut the baking time in half.

BARBECUE BAKED BEANS

SERVES 6 ■ PREP TIME: 15 MINUTES ■ COOK TIME: 20 MINUTES

GF DF

3 bacon slices, cut into pieces

1 onion, chopped

3 garlic cloves, minced

1 (14-ounce) can black
soybeans, drained

1 cup Barbecue Sauce (page 168)

PER SERVING
Calories: 332; Total carbs: 24g;
Net carbs: 17g; Fiber: 7g; Fat: 15g;
Protein: 26g; Sodium: 289mg

This perfect picnic side is a little sweet, a little savory, and a little smoky. That's what makes it so tempting. This dish is typically made with starchy high-carb beans, but black soybeans are used here to reduce carbohydrate levels significantly.

1 In a medium pot over medium-high heat, cook the bacon for about 5 minutes, or until crispy.

2 Add the onion. Cook for 3 to 4 minutes, stirring frequently, until soft.

3 Stir in the garlic, black soybeans, and Barbecue Sauce. Reduce the heat to medium-low.

4 Simmer for about 10 minutes, stirring frequently, until the flavors meld and the beans are heated through, and serve.

SAUSAGE STUFFING

SERVES 4 ■ PREP TIME: 15 MINUTES ■ COOK TIME: 40 MINUTES

GF

½ pound pork sausage

½ onion, finely chopped

1 celery stalk, finely chopped

4 garlic cloves, minced

1 cup chopped cauliflower

4 ounces mushrooms, chopped

1 large egg, beaten

2 tablespoons unsalted butter, melted and cooled slightly

2 ounces Asiago cheese, grated

1 tablespoon chopped fresh Italian parsley

1 tablespoon dried sage

1 tablespoon dried thyme

½ teaspoon salt

¼ teaspoon freshly ground black pepper

PER SERVING
Calories: 336; Total carbs: 6g;
Net carbs: 4g; Fiber: 2g; Fat: 27g;
Protein: 18g; Sodium: 920mg

If tonight's dinner is roast chicken, turkey, or even roast beef, stuffing is a perfect—carb-laden—side dish. No need to change the menu, though. You can still get the stuffing flavor, without the bread and carbs, by changing a few simple ingredients.

1 Preheat the oven to 350°F.

2 In a large skillet over medium-high heat, cook the sausage for about 5 minutes, crumbling with a spoon, until browned.

3 Add the onion and celery. Cook for about 3 minutes more, stirring occasionally, until the vegetables are soft.

4 Add the garlic. Cook for 30 to 60 seconds, stirring constantly, until fragrant. Remove from the heat. Allow to cool slightly.

5 In a large bowl, combine the cauliflower, onion and sausage mixture, mushrooms, egg, butter, Asiago cheese, parsley, sage, thyme, salt, and pepper. Mix well.

6 Transfer the mixture to a 9-inch square baking dish. Bake for about 30 minutes, or until browned, and serve.

WHY IT WORKS: Let's face it—the bread in stuffing is filler and really provides a backdrop for all the other fabulous flavors. This stuffing has those flavors but uses cauliflower as its backdrop instead.

SNACKS

HUMMUS

SERVES 4 ▪ PREP TIME: 5 MINUTES

GF V DF

- 2 garlic cloves, chopped
- 1 zucchini, peeled and cut into pieces
- ¼ cup tahini
- 2 tablespoons extra-virgin olive oil, plus additional for drizzling
- 2 tablespoons freshly squeezed lemon juice
- 1 teaspoon ground cumin
- ½ teaspoon salt
- 2 red bell peppers, seeded and sliced, or other sliced veggies, for dipping

PER SERVING
Calories: 172; Total carbs: 8g; Net carbs: 5g; Fiber: 2g; Fat: 15g; Protein: 4g; Sodium: 318mg

Hummus is addictive! Made with flavorful spices like cumin and garlic, scented with lemon juice and tahini, and blended with olive oil, traditional chickpea hummus hits all the taste buds, making it very craveable. Chickpeas, however, are very starchy and high in carbs. Fortunately, their neutral flavor can easily be replaced with lower-carb ingredients—here, zucchini—so you can still indulge in this Mediterranean delight.

1 In a food processor fitted with a chopping blade, pulse the garlic until minced. Using a rubber spatula, scrape down the sides of the bowl.

2 Add the zucchini, tahini, olive oil, lemon juice, cumin, and salt. Process until smooth.

3 Serve drizzled with olive oil, accompanied by the red bell peppers for dipping.

SHRIMP COCKTAIL

SERVES 2 ▪ PREP TIME: 5 MINUTES, PLUS 30 MINUTES CHILLING TIME

8 ounces cooked baby shrimp
1 celery stalk, minced
¼ cup Cocktail Sauce (page 169)

PER SERVING
Calories: 98; Total carbs: 5g;
Net carbs: 4g; Fiber: 1g; Fat: 1g;
Protein: 20g; Sodium: 963mg

Delightful shrimp cocktail is light, sweet, and slightly salty. The tender shrimp are combined with crunchy celery for a mouth-pleasing texture. Cocktail sauce typically contains sugar, which makes it higher in carbs than is ideal on a low-carb diet. Use low-carb Cocktail Sauce (page 169) for all of the flavor and spice without the carbs.

1 In a small bowl, mix together the shrimp, celery, and Cocktail Sauce.

2 Divide evenly between 2 serving dishes or martini glasses.

3 Chill for 30 minutes before serving.

NACHOS

SERVES 4 ▪ PREP TIME: 10 MINUTES ▪ COOK TIME: 25 MINUTES, PLUS 45 MINUTES COOLING TIME

GF V

FOR THE CHIPS

Cooking spray

16 ounces pepper Jack cheese, grated

2 ounces Parmesan cheese, grated

½ teaspoon garlic powder

½ teaspoon ground cumin

¼ teaspoon chipotle chili powder

FOR THE GUACAMOLE

1 avocado

2 tablespoons freshly squeezed lime juice

¼ red onion, minced

1 garlic clove, minced

1 tablespoon chopped fresh cilantro

¼ teaspoon salt

FOR THE NACHOS

¼ cup pickled jalapeño pepper slices

3 scallions, chopped

1 tomato, diced

4 ounces grated Cheddar cheese

½ cup sour cream

½ cup salsa

PER SERVING
Calories: 798; Total carbs: 12g;
Net carbs: 7g; Fiber: 5g; Fat: 65g;
Protein: 43g; Sodium: 1,483mg

Who doesn't love cheesy, spicy, gooey nachos? The biggest issue with nachos for people on low-carb diets is the tortilla chips, which are made from high-carb corn. This version uses chips made from cheese, with more cheese and other toppings piled on top. The result is gooey, tasty, cheesy nachos, without the corn or carbs.

TO MAKE THE CHIPS

1 Preheat the oven to 400°F.

2 Line a baking sheet with parchment paper. Spray with nonstick cooking spray. Set aside.

3 In a medium bowl, mix together the pepper Jack cheese, Parmesan cheese, garlic powder, cumin, and chili powder.

4 Spread the mixture on the prepared sheet. Bake for 8 to 10 minutes, or until the cheese is browned around the edges. Check frequently to ensure that it does not burn.

5 Remove from the oven. Let cool for 15 minutes.

6 Preheat the broiler.

7 Peel away the cheese crisp from the parchment. Cut the crisp into chip-size pieces.

8 Return the chips to the baking sheet. Place the sheet under the broiler for about 2 minutes to crisp.

9 Remove from the oven. Let cool for 30 minutes.

TO MAKE THE GUACAMOLE

Just before the nachos are ready to come out of the oven, in a small bowl, mash together the avocado, lime juice, red onion, garlic, cilantro, and salt with a fork.

1 Preheat the oven to 425°F.

2 Put the chips in a 9-inch square baking dish.

3 Top with the jalapeños, scallions, and tomatoes, and sprinkle with the grated Cheddar cheese.

4 Bake for 10 minutes, or until the cheese melts.

5 Serve with the sour cream, salsa, and guacamole on the side for dipping.

TIMESAVING TIP: Instead of baking the nachos to melt the Cheddar cheese, arrange them on a microwave-safe plate and microwave for about 1 minute on high.

QUESADILLAS

SERVES 2 ▪ PREP TIME: 5 MINUTES ▪ COOK TIME: 10 MINUTES

V

2 tablespoons unsalted butter

2 low-carb tortillas

4 ounces pepper Jack
   cheese, grated

¼ cup salsa

¼ cup sour cream

PER SERVING
Calories: 433; Total carbs: 16g;
Net carbs: 9g; Fiber: 7g; Fat: 31g;
Protein: 22g; Sodium: 1,044mg

Craving those southwest flavors? Quesadillas are simple to make and deliver a big flavor payoff with their gooey melted cheese. Cut this low-carb version into wedges and dip into salsa and sour cream for a taste that is delicious.

1 In a large nonstick skillet over medium-high heat, melt the butter.

2 Add 1 tortilla to the skillet. Top with the cheese and then the remaining tortilla.

3 Cook for about 4 minutes, or until browned on the bottom.

4 Flip the quesadilla. Cook for about 4 minutes more, or until browned on the second side.

5 Cut into 4 wedges, and serve with the salsa and sour cream for dipping.

WHY IT WORKS: Low-carb tortillas are a fantastic substitute for their higher-carb brethren. While they are not gluten-free, they do offer flavors similar to regular tortillas without all the carbs. Eat them sparingly, however, as they do contain some carbs.

SPINACH AND ARTICHOKE DIP

SERVES 4 ▪ PREP TIME: 5 MINUTES ▪ COOK TIME: 35 MINUTES

GF V

4 ounces cream cheese,
   at room temperature

2 tablespoons sour cream

2 tablespoons mayonnaise

1 teaspoon garlic powder

½ teaspoon chili powder

½ cup chopped spinach

1 (14-ounce) jar marinated
   artichoke hearts, drained
   and chopped

8 ounces Parmesan
   cheese, grated

PER SERVING
Calories: 342; Total carbs: 9g;
Net carbs: 8g; Fiber: 1g; Fat: 26g;
Protein: 22g; Sodium: 842mg

Where's the party? Loaded with melty, gooey cheese, this dip keeps you coming back for more. Dip anything you like in this: Celery tastes as good as baked low-carb tortilla chips. Let your choices help control your carbs.

1 Preheat the oven to 350°F.

2 In a large bowl, mix together the cream cheese, sour cream, mayonnaise, garlic powder, and chili powder until well combined.

3 Stir in the spinach, artichokes, and Parmesan cheese until well combined.

4 Transfer the mixture to a 9-inch square baking dish. Bake for about 35 minutes, or until the dip is warm, bubbly, and browned on top.

5 Serve with low-carb tortilla chips and/or the veggies of your choice.

TIMESAVING TIP: In a microwave-safe bowl, mix together all the ingredients except the Parmesan cheese. Microwave for about 3 minutes on high, or until the mixture is warm and bubbly. Transfer it to a 9-inch square baking dish, and top with the Parmesan cheese. Broil for 2 or 3 minutes, or until the cheese is brown and bubbly.

FRIED ZUCCHINI WITH RANCH DRESSING

SERVES 2 ▪ PREP TIME: 5 MINUTES, PLUS 20 MINUTES TO DRAIN ▪ COOK TIME: 5 MINUTES

`GF` `V`

2 medium zucchini, halved cross-wise, then cut into wedges

1 tablespoon salt

Coconut oil, for frying

2 large eggs

½ cup Parmesan cheese, grated

¼ cup almond meal

½ teaspoon freshly ground black pepper

½ teaspoon garlic powder

½ cup Ranch Dressing (page 167)

PER SERVING
Calories: 664; Total carbs: 18g; Net carbs: 14g; Fiber: 4g; Fat: 26g; Protein: 48g; Sodium: 1,473mg

Who doesn't love fried zucchini? With its crisp and salty coating of cheese and bread crumbs and its tender, soft insides, it's a really tasty savory snack. Well, meet the carb-friendly version you can love, too. Almond meal stands in for bread crumbs to cut carbs. Ranch Dressing (page 167) perfectly complements the dish with the taste of cool herbs. Get ready to be amazed with flavor.

1 In a colander set over a bowl or the sink, sprinkle the zucchini with the salt. Let sit for about 20 minutes to allow the salt to draw out the water.

2 Using paper towels, wipe the salt from the zucchini and pat dry.

3 In a large pot over medium-high heat, heat 1 inch of oil until it reaches 350°F.

4 Line a plate with paper towels.

5 In a small bowl, whisk the eggs.

6 In a medium bowl, whisk together the Parmesan cheese, almond meal, pepper, and garlic powder.

7 Working one at a time, dip the zucchini wedges into the eggs, and then into the almond meal and cheese mixture.

8 Drop the zucchini pieces into the hot oil. Fry for about 5 minutes, or until browned.

9 Using a skimmer or slotted spoon, carefully transfer the zucchini from the oil to the paper towel–lined plate.

10 Serve hot with Ranch Dressing for dipping.

WHY IT WORKS: Drawing the water out of the zucchini with the salt makes it easier to fry because the water doesn't dilute the oil. Parmesan cheese and almond meal in place of bread crumbs make a low-carb, crispy coating.

FRENCH FRIES

SERVES 2 ▪ PREP TIME: 10 MINUTES ▪ COOK TIME: 20 MINUTES

3 large carrots, julienned
Coconut oil, for frying
½ teaspoon salt

PER SERVING
Calories: 164; Total carbs: 11g;
Net carbs: 8g; Fiber: 3g; Fat: 14g;
Protein: 1g; Sodium: 656mg

There's just something about French fries that makes them really hard to give up. Perhaps it's the salty, crispy exterior, or maybe it's the warm, soft interior. Whatever it is, they are made from starchy potatoes loaded with carbs. Substituting another starchy veggie with fewer carbs is the best way to get the texture and flavor of fries without the diet-busting carbohydrates.

1 Set a large pot filled with water over high heat. Bring to a boil.

2 Add the carrots, and blanch for 5 minutes.

3 Drain the carrots, and run cold water over them to stop the cooking. Transfer the carrots to paper towels, and blot them dry.

4 In a large pot over medium-high heat, heat 1 inch of oil until it reaches 375°F.

5 Line a platter with paper towels.

6 Working in two or three batches so you don't crowd the pot, fry the carrots for about 5 minutes, or until they turn a deep rust color. Using a skimmer or slotted spoon, carefully transfer them from the hot oil onto the paper towel–lined platter.

7 Sprinkle with salt, and serve.

TRY IT THIS WAY: If you have a spiral slicer, spiralizing the carrots is a great way to get them into julienne shapes. Use the spaghetti blade, and cut long spirals in half.

ONION RINGS

SERVES 4 ■ PREP TIME: 10 MINUTES ■ COOK TIME: 35 MINUTES

GF DF

1 medium onion, sliced and
    separated into rings
2 large eggs, beaten
½ cup almond flour
½ cup crushed pork rinds
Pinch cayenne pepper
¼ teaspoon salt

PER SERVING
Calories: 141; Total carbs: 3g;
Net carbs: 2g; Fiber: 1g; Fat: 9g;
Protein: 13g; Sodium: 452mg

Onion rings are savory and delicious, whether you serve them as a side dish or to top off a tasty burger. Their typical coating is made with beer and wheat flour, which ups the carbs. Using pork rinds and almond meal makes a delicious crust that allows you to bake the onion rings with far fewer carbs to keep your diet on target.

1 Preheat the oven to 350°F.

2 Line a baking sheet with parchment paper.

3 In a large bowl, toss the onions with the beaten eggs.

4 In a small bowl, whisk together the almond flour, pork rinds, cayenne pepper, and salt.

5 Remove the onion rings from the eggs one at a time, allowing any excess egg to drip away. Dip each ring in the pork rind and almond flour mixture, coating it completely. Put the coated ring on the prepared sheet. As you add more, keep them in a single layer.

6 Bake for 30 to 35 minutes, or until the crust is golden, and serve hot.

WHY IT WORKS: The pork rinds have enough fat in them to help form a crust, giving the onion rings the same texture as traditional fried onion rings.

CHEESE STICKS WITH MARINARA

SERVES 4 ▪ PREP TIME: 10 MINUTES ▪ COOK TIME: 30 MINUTES, PLUS 30 MINUTES FREEZING TIME

GF

FOR THE MARINARA

2 tablespoons extra-virgin olive oil

½ onion, minced

3 garlic cloves, minced

1 (14-ounce) can crushed tomatoes, undrained

½ teaspoon salt

2 tablespoons chopped fresh basil

FOR THE CHEESE STICKS

½ cup Parmesan cheese

¼ cup almond flour

¼ cup crushed pork rinds

½ teaspoon garlic powder

¼ teaspoon freshly ground black pepper

2 large eggs, beaten

6 pieces full-fat string cheese, halved crosswise

Fat or oil, such as lard or coconut oil, for frying

PER SERVING
Calories: 530; Total carbs: 14g; Net carbs: 10g; Fiber: 4g; Fat: 36g; Protein: 42g; Sodium: 1,649mg

Do you ever just crave cheese, melted inside a browned and tasty batter? The thought may evoke images of dining in a little café or Italian restaurant. With a few tweaks to the recipe, you can enjoy the flavorful goodness of cheese sticks once again, checkered tablecloth optional.

TO MAKE THE MARINARA

1 In a medium pot over medium-high heat, heat the olive oil until it shimmers.

2 Add the onion. Cook for about 5 minutes, stirring occasionally, until soft.

3 Add the garlic. Cook for 30 to 60 seconds, stirring constantly, until fragrant.

4 Stir in the tomatoes and the salt. Reduce the heat to medium. Cook for about 15 minutes, stirring occasionally, until the liquid evaporates and the sauce thickens.

5 Stir in the basil. Remove from the heat. Set aside.

TO MAKE THE CHEESE STICKS

1 Line a tray with parchment paper.

2 In a small bowl, whisk together the Parmesan cheese, almond flour, pork rinds, garlic powder, and pepper.

3 In a small bowl, whisk the eggs.

4 Working one at a time, dip the cheese sticks in the eggs, and then in the almond flour and pork rind mixture. Put them on the prepared tray and into the freezer for 30 minutes.

5 In a large pot over medium-high heat, heat 1 inch of oil until it reaches 375°F on a candy thermometer.

6 Fry the cheese sticks in the hot oil for 5 to 10 minutes, or until golden. Serve hot with the marinara for dipping.

STUFFED MUSHROOMS

SERVES 4 ▪ PREP TIME: 10 MINUTES ▪ COOK TIME: 55 MINUTES

GF

12 large button mushrooms, gently wiped clean, stemmed, stems chopped and reserved

2 tablespoons extra-virgin olive oil

¾ pound Italian sausage

½ onion, minced

½ teaspoon salt

3 garlic cloves, minced

¼ cup almond flour

¼ cup crushed pork rinds

2 tablespoons chopped fresh Italian parsley

4 ounces grated Parmesan cheese

PER SERVING
Calories: 595; Total carbs: 6g; Net carbs: 5g; Fiber: 1g; Fat: 46g; Protein: 42g; Sodium: 1,608mg

Warm mushrooms filled with a tasty stuffing offer the perfect bite-size craving buster. When working with mushrooms, don't rinse them with water to clean them because the mushrooms will soak up the water. Instead, wipe them gently with a dry paper towel.

1 Preheat the oven to 325°F.

2 Line a baking sheet with parchment paper.

3 In a medium bowl, toss the mushroom caps with the olive oil. Set aside.

4 In a large skillet over medium-high heat, cook the sausage for about 5 minutes, crumbling with a spoon, until browned.

5 Add the onion, reserved mushroom stems, and salt. Cook for about 5 minutes more, stirring occasionally, until the vegetables are soft.

6 Add the garlic. Cook for 30 to 60 seconds, stirring constantly, until fragrant.

7 Stir in the almond flour, pork rinds, parsley, and Parmesan cheese. Remove the mixture from the heat.

8 Transfer the mushroom caps to the prepared baking sheet, stem-side up.

9 Spoon the sausage mixture evenly into the caps.

10 Bake for about 40 minutes, or until the mushrooms are soft and cooked.

FRIED COCONUT SHRIMP

SERVES 4 ▪ PREP TIME: 10 MINUTES ▪ COOK TIME: 20 MINUTES

Coconut oil, for frying

1 cup unsweetened coconut flakes

4 large eggs, beaten

5 tablespoons coconut flour

½ teaspoon baking powder

½ teaspoon salt

⅛ teaspoon freshly ground
    black pepper

16 large shrimp, peeled,
    deveined, and tails removed

PER SERVING
Calories: 374; Total carbs: 13g;
Net carbs: 4g; Fiber: 9g; Fat: 29g;
Protein: 14g; Sodium: 435mg

The tropical flavor of coconut pairs wonderfully with sweet, succulent shrimp meat. Typical coconut shrimp comes in a high-carb crust that puts it out of bounds for most low-carbers. If you've been craving coconut shrimp, this recipe is perfectly in bounds for you.

1 In a large pot over medium-high heat, heat at least 1 inch of coconut oil until it reaches 350°F on a candy thermometer.

2 Line a tray with paper towels.

3 To a medium bowl, add the coconut flakes.

4 In another medium bowl, whisk together the eggs, coconut flour, baking powder, salt, and pepper.

5 Dip the shrimp in the egg batter.

6 Dip the battered shrimp in the coconut flakes.

7 Working in two or three batches, fry the shrimp in the hot oil for about 4 minutes per side, or until they are golden brown on both sides.

8 Transfer the shrimp to the paper towels to drain before serving.

BUFFALO CHICKEN WINGS WITH BLUE CHEESE DRESSING

SERVES 4 ▪ PREP TIME: 10 MINUTES ▪ COOK TIME: 45 MINUTES

GF

2 pounds chicken wings, tips removed and separated into pieces

2 tablespoons extra-virgin olive oil

½ teaspoon salt

¼ teaspoon freshly ground black pepper

½ cup (1 stick) unsalted butter, melted

½ cup Louisiana hot sauce

4 celery stalks, halved lengthwise and then cut into thirds crosswise

¼ cup Blue Cheese Dressing (page 166)

PER SERVING
Calories: 781; Total carbs: 3g;
Net carbs: 2g; Fiber: 1g; Fat: 55g;
Protein: 67g; Sodium: 1,610mg

Cool and salty Blue Cheese Dressing (page 166) is the perfect accompaniment to the spicy sauce on these buffalo wings. The buffalo sauce, made from a Louisiana hot sauce such as Frank's RedHot and melted butter, is quite low in carbs. It's the breading on the wings that adds the carbs. This recipe delivers all the flavor in a finger-licking carb-friendly package.

1 Preheat the oven to 400°F.

2 Put a large wire rack on top of a rimmed baking sheet.

3 In a large bowl, toss the chicken wings with the olive oil, salt, and pepper.

4 Put the wings on the baking rack. Bake for about 45 minutes, or until the wings are crispy.

5 In a large bowl, whisk together the butter and Louisiana hot sauce. Add the hot wings, and toss to coat.

6 Serve with the celery sticks and the Blue Cheese Dressing for dipping.

TIMESAVING TIP: You can deep fry the chicken wings for 15 to 20 minutes in coconut oil heated to 350°F instead of baking them for 45 minutes.

CHICKEN FINGERS

SERVES 4 ▪ PREP TIME: 10 MINUTES ▪ COOK TIME: 35 MINUTES

GF

½ cup grated Parmesan cheese

¼ cup crushed pork rinds

¼ cup almond flour

1 teaspoon dried thyme

1 tablespoon paprika

½ teaspoon salt

¼ teaspoon freshly ground
   black pepper

½ cup (1 stick) unsalted
   butter, melted

2 pounds chicken breast tenders

PER SERVING
Calories: 726; Total carbs: 4g;
Net carbs: 3g; Fiber: 1g; Fat: 45g;
Protein: 77g; Sodium: 1,838mg

These crispy chicken fingers have all the flavor of the commercially prepared varieties but only a fraction of the carbs. The exteriors have a crispy, salty crunch, while the insides are tender and juicy, just the way you crave them. Serve these with Ranch Dressing (page 167), Blue Cheese Dressing (page 166), or Barbecue Sauce (page 168), and feel like a kid again.

1 Preheat the oven to 350°F.

2 Line a baking sheet with parchment paper.

3 In a large bowl, whisk together the Parmesan cheese, pork rinds, almond flour, thyme, paprika, salt, and pepper.

4 To a large bowl, add the melted butter.

5 Dip the chicken tenders in the butter and then in the cheese and pork rind mixture. Place them on the prepared baking sheet in a single layer.

6 Bake for about 35 minutes, or until the chicken is cooked through, and serve.

SWEDISH MEATBALLS

SERVES 4 ■ PREP TIME: 10 MINUTES ■ COOK TIME: 25 MINUTES

GF

- ½ pound ground beef
- ½ pound ground pork
- ¼ cup almond flour
- ¼ cup crushed pork rinds
- ¼ onion, grated
- 1 large egg
- ¼ teaspoon ground allspice
- 1 teaspoon salt, divided
- ½ teaspoon freshly ground black pepper, divided
- 2 tablespoons butter
- 1½ cups unsalted beef broth
- 1 cup sour cream
- ½ cup heavy (whipping) cream
- 1 tablespoon chopped fresh parsley

PER SERVING
Calories: 726; Total carbs: 4g; Net carbs: 3g; Fiber: 1g; Fat: 45g; Protein: 77g; Sodium: 1,838mg

It seems as if this perennial party favorite is everywhere. The savory meatballs in a creamy sauce are perfect for eating by themselves or spooned atop a starchy purée like Mashed Potatoes (page 45). Whether you plan to eat them as a snack or take them to a party, these flavorful carb-friendly meatballs are sure to satisfy and liven things up.

1 In a large bowl, using your hands, mix the beef, pork, almond flour, pork rinds, onion, egg, allspice, ½ teaspoon of salt, and ¼ teaspoon of pepper until well combined. Form the mixture into 1-inch meatballs.

2 In a large skillet over medium-high heat, heat the butter.

3 Add the meatballs to the skillet. Work in batches if necessary to avoid overcrowding the pan. Cook for about 10 minutes, turning occasionally, until the meatballs are cooked through. Transfer the meatballs to a dish. Set aside.

4 With the skillet still on medium-high heat, add the beef broth, scraping up any browned bits from the bottom. Bring to a boil. Add the remaining ½ teaspoon of salt and ¼ teaspoon of pepper.

5 Whisk in the sour cream and heavy cream. Reduce the heat to low. Cook for 3 to 4 minutes, stirring constantly, until the sauce thickens.

6 Stir in the meatballs and parsley, and serve.

WHY IT WORKS: Normally, carb-carrying bread crumbs lighten the meatballs. In this case, lower-carb pork rinds and almond flour step in for the bread crumbs, keeping the meatballs from becoming overly heavy and dense.

POT STICKERS WITH DIPPING SAUCE

SERVES 4 ▪ PREP TIME: 10 MINUTES ▪ COOK TIME: 20 MINUTES

DF

FOR THE DIPPING SAUCE

¼ cup soy sauce

¼ cup rice vinegar

¼ teaspoon chili oil

½ packet stevia

FOR THE POT STICKERS

1 pound ground pork

3 scallions, minced

½ tablespoon minced
   fresh ginger

3 garlic cloves, minced

2 tablespoons chopped
   fresh cilantro

½ cup almond meal

1 cup finely chopped cabbage

1 teaspoon salt

2 large eggs, beaten

8 large lettuce leaves

PER SERVING
Calories: 301; Total carbs: 8g;
Net carbs: 5g; Fiber: 3g; Fat: 13g;
Protein: 37g; Sodium: 1,583mg

At Chinese restaurants and beyond, savory pot stickers are a popular appetizer. Part of what makes them delicious is the flavorful ground pork mixture stuffed in the middle. What makes them truly spectacular, however, is how well the pot sticker filling blends with the flavorful dipping sauce. Skip the tempting takeout, and try these instead.

TO MAKE THE DIPPING SAUCE

In a small bowl, whisk together the soy sauce, rice vinegar, chili oil, and stevia. Set aside.

TO MAKE THE POT STICKERS

1 Preheat the oven to 400°F.

2 Line a 9-by-13-inch baking dish with parchment paper.

3 In a large bowl, mix the pork, scallions, ginger, garlic, cilantro, almond meal, cabbage, salt, and eggs until well combined. Roll into 1-inch balls, and put the balls in the prepared dish.

4 Bake for about 20 minutes, or until cooked through.

5 Wrap the pork balls in the lettuce leaves, and serve with the dipping sauce.

WHY IT WORKS: The texture of the traditional pot sticker wrapper is nice, but it doesn't contribute anything to the flavor. Using lettuce in its place allows you to get all the flavors of the filling combined with the flavorful dipping sauce, without all the usual carbs.

SOUPS, STEWS, AND CHILIES

CHICKEN NOODLE SOUP

SERVES 4 ■ PREP TIME: 10 MINUTES ■ COOK TIME: 15 MINUTES

GF DF

- 2 medium zucchini
- 2 tablespoons extra-virgin olive oil
- 1 onion, chopped
- 2 carrots, chopped
- 2 celery stalks, chopped
- 3 garlic cloves, minced
- 5 cups unsalted chicken broth
- 1 pound cooked chicken meat, cut into pieces
- 1 teaspoon dried thyme
- ½ teaspoon salt
- ¼ teaspoon freshly ground black pepper

PER SERVING
Calories: 351; Total carbs: 12g;
Net carbs: 9g; Fiber: 3g; Fat: 16g;
Protein: 40g; Sodium: 293mg

There's nothing better than a hot bowl of chicken noodle soup on a cool night. Of course, chicken noodle soup is also the go-to meal when you aren't feeling well. Is it any wonder that so many people crave its comforting warmth and aromas? Don't worry about the carbs. Zucchini stands in for the noodles here.

1 Using a vegetable peeler, cut the zucchini into ribbons. Then cut the ribbons into noodle-size strips. Set aside.

2 In a large pot over medium-high heat, heat the olive oil until it shimmers.

3 Add the onion, carrots, and celery. Cook for 6 to 7 minutes, stirring occasionally, until the vegetables are soft and start to brown.

4 Add the garlic. Cook for 30 to 60 seconds, stirring constantly, until fragrant.

5 Stir in the chicken broth, chicken meat, thyme, salt, and pepper. Bring to a simmer. Reduce the heat to medium.

6 Add the zucchini. Cook for about 5 minutes, or until the zucchini is soft, and serve.

TRY IT THIS WAY: You can spiralize the zucchini into spaghetti noodles (leave the skin on). You can also use a mandoline on the julienne setting.

TORTILLA SOUP

SERVES 4 ■ PREP TIME: 15 MINUTES ■ COOK TIME: 40 MINUTES

1 low-carb tortilla

2 tablespoons extra-virgin olive oil

1 onion, chopped

2 jalapeño peppers, seeded and minced

4 garlic cloves, minced

6 cups chicken broth

1 (14-ounce) can tomatoes with green chiles, such as Ro-Tel

8 ounces boneless, skinless chicken breast

2 carrots, diced

1 teaspoon salt

⅛ teaspoon freshly ground black pepper

Juice of 2 limes

½ cup chopped fresh cilantro

1 avocado, peeled, pitted, and cubed, divided

1 cup shredded pepper Jack cheese, divided

PER SERVING
Calories: 817; Total carbs: 25g;
Net carbs: 15g; Fiber: 3g; Fat: 10g;
Protein: 51g; Sodium: 2,726mg

If you crave it, you can have it. Tortilla soup, with shredded chicken and savory southwestern flavors, offers a spicy twist on traditional chicken soup. If you like your tortilla soup on the milder side, use regular canned tomatoes instead of the canned tomatoes with green chiles, and dial back on the jalapeños.

1 In a dry skillet over medium-high heat, toast the tortilla for about 4 minutes per side, or until slightly crispy on both sides. Cut the tortilla into strips. Set aside.

2 In a large pot over medium-high heat, heat the olive oil until it shimmers.

3 Add the onion and jalapeños. Cook for 6 to 7 minutes, stirring occasionally, until the vegetables are soft and start to brown.

4 Add the garlic. Cook for 30 to 60 seconds, stirring constantly, until fragrant.

5 Add the chicken broth and tomatoes with green chiles. Bring to a boil. Reduce the heat to medium.

6 Add the chicken, carrots, salt, and pepper. Cook for about 25 minutes, stirring occasionally, until the chicken is cooked through.

7 Remove the chicken from the broth, and shred it with a fork. Portion the shredded chicken and reserved tortilla strips among 4 bowls.

8 Add the lime juice and cilantro to the pot, and stir to combine. Remove the soup from the heat.

9 Ladle the soup over the chicken and tortilla strips.

10 Garnish each dish with one-quarter of the avocado and ¼ cup of pepper Jack cheese, and serve.

CHEDDAR-BROCCOLI SOUP

SERVES 4 ▪ PREP TIME: 5 MINUTES ▪ COOK TIME: 25 MINUTES

GF V

2 tablespoons unsalted butter

1 onion, chopped

3 garlic cloves, minced

2 cups unsalted vegetable broth

4 cups broccoli florets

¾ cup heavy (whipping) cream

3 cups grated sharp
Cheddar cheese

½ teaspoon salt

¼ teaspoon freshly ground
black pepper

PER SERVING
Calories: 535; Total carbs: 12g;
Net carbs: 9g; Fiber: 3g; Fat: 43g;
Protein: 27g; Sodium: 1,280mg

Cheddar-broccoli soup is a warm, satisfying comfort food that also offers one of the tastiest ways to eat broccoli. This low-carb version lets you indulge in all the flavor of the original. A fantastic cravings buster on its own, this soup also goes great with a low-carb sandwich like the French Dip (page 93).

1 In a large pot over medium-high heat, heat the butter.

2 Add the onion. Cook for about 5 minutes, stirring occasionally, until soft.

3 Add the garlic. Cook for 30 to 60 seconds, stirring constantly, until fragrant.

4 Add the vegetable broth and the broccoli. Bring to a boil. Reduce the heat to medium. Cover and simmer for about 10 minutes, or until the broccoli is tender.

5 Stir in the heavy cream. Simmer for 3 to 4 minutes, stirring constantly, until the cream is hot.

6 Add the Cheddar cheese. Stir constantly for 3 to 4 minutes, until the cheese melts and is incorporated into the soup.

7 Season with salt and pepper, and serve.

WHY IT WORKS: Traditional broccoli-cheese soup starts with a béchamel sauce, which is made from flour and half-and-half. While the béchamel thickens the soup, it doesn't really add any flavor to it, so it is easily replaced with a lower-carb ingredient. In this case, heavy cream replaces the béchamel, reducing the carb count significantly without sacrificing any of the flavor.

CREAM OF MUSHROOM SOUP

SERVES 4 ▪ PREP TIME: 10 MINUTES, PLUS 3 HOURS TO SOAK ▪ COOK TIME: 15 MINUTES

GF V

4 cups unsalted vegetable broth

2 ounces dried porcini mushrooms

2 tablespoons unsalted butter

1 onion, chopped

1 pound cremini
    mushrooms, sliced

3 garlic cloves, minced

1 teaspoon dried thyme

¾ teaspoon salt

¼ teaspoon freshly ground
    black pepper

1½ cups heavy (whipping) cream

PER SERVING
Calories: 343; Total carbs: 17g;
Net carbs: 12g; Fiber: 5g; Fat: 24g;
Protein: 13g; Sodium: 1,268mg

Mushrooms have an important flavor profile known as umami. Umami, one of the five types of taste your tongue can distinguish, is a deeply savory flavor. This mushroom soup makeover is loaded with umami flavor in a rich and creamy broth.

1 In a medium pot over medium-high heat, bring the vegetable broth to a boil. Remove from the heat. Add the porcini mushrooms. Cover and let soak for 3 hours.

2 Remove the porcini mushrooms from the broth, reserving the broth. Roughly chop the mushrooms.

3 In a large pot over medium-high heat, heat the butter.

4 Add the onion, cremini mushrooms, and chopped porcini mushrooms. Cook for about 7 minutes, stirring occasionally, until the vegetables brown.

5 Add the garlic. Cook for 30 to 60 seconds, stirring constantly, until fragrant.

6 Add the reserved broth, thyme, salt, and pepper. Bring to a boil. Reduce the heat to medium.

7 Stir in the heavy cream. Cook for about 3 minutes more, stirring constantly, until the cream is hot, and serve.

WHY IT WORKS: Soaking the dried porcini mushrooms infuses the broth with the savory mushroom flavor that then flavors the soup much more deeply than if you had used fresh mushrooms alone.

NEW ENGLAND CLAM CHOWDER

SERVES 4 ▪ PREP TIME: 10 MINUTES ▪ COOK TIME: 20 MINUTES

GF

4 slices thick-cut pepper bacon,
   cut into pieces
1 onion, chopped
2 carrots, chopped
1 red bell pepper, chopped
1 fennel bulb, chopped
3 garlic cloves, minced
5 cups unsalted chicken broth
2 medium zucchini, cut into chunks
8 ounces clam meat,
   canned or fresh
1 teaspoon dried thyme
1/8 teaspoon red pepper flakes
1 1/2 cups heavy (whipping) cream
1/2 teaspoon salt
1/4 teaspoon freshly ground
   black pepper

PER SERVING
Calories: 329; Total carbs: 21g;
Net carbs: 16g; Fiber: 5g; Fat: 20g;
Protein: 20g; Sodium: 665mg

Creamy and a little salty, New England clam chowder is the perfect lunch on a chilly afternoon. It's loaded with chunks of vegetables and sweet clams in a deeply satisfying creamy broth, with a slightly smoky blend of flavors. Your low-carb diet is safe with this catch of the day!

1 In a large pot over medium-high heat, cook the bacon for 5 minutes, stirring frequently, until browned.

2 Using a slotted spoon, remove it from the rendered fat and set aside on a paper towel–lined plate.

3 To the fat remaining in the pan, add the onion, carrots, red bell pepper, and fennel. Cook for 6 to 8 minutes, stirring occasionally, until the vegetables soften and brown.

4 Add the garlic. Cook for 30 to 60 seconds, stirring constantly, until fragrant.

5 Stir in the chicken broth, zucchini, clam meat, thyme, and red pepper flakes. Bring to a boil. Reduce the heat to medium. Cook for about 6 minutes, or until the zucchini is soft.

6 Stir in the heavy cream, reserved bacon, salt, and pepper. Cook for about 3 minutes more, stirring constantly, until the cream is hot, and serve.

WHY IT WORKS: Clam chowder gets its flavor from the bacon, clams, aromatic vegetables, and herbs—all elements that remain in this recipe. Instead of starchy potatoes, however, zucchini fills in. Likewise, heavy cream replaces the bacon grease and white flour roux that usually thickens the soup.

CHILI CON CARNE

SERVES 4 ▪ PREP TIME: 10 MINUTES ▪ COOK TIME: 15 MINUTES

GF

½ pound ground beef

1 onion, chopped

1 green bell pepper, chopped

4 garlic cloves, minced

1 cup black soybeans, drained

1 (15-ounce) can crushed tomatoes, undrained

1 cup unsalted beef broth

2 tablespoons chili powder

⅛ teaspoon cayenne pepper

½ teaspoon ground cumin

½ teaspoon dried oregano

½ teaspoon salt

¼ teaspoon freshly ground black pepper

8 ounces Monterey Jack cheese, grated

8 scallions, chopped

PER SERVING
Calories: 612; Total carbs: 32g;
Net carbs: 22g; Fiber: 10g; Fat: 31g;
Protein: 53g; Sodium: 915mg

A spicy bowl of chili is both flavorful and satisfying. The starchy beans soak up the flavor of the chili spices, while ground beef and tomatoes make the dish hearty and flavorful. When topped with chopped scallions and grated cheese, it's a perfect meal. Spice up your next tailgate party with this lower-carb version.

1 In a large pot over medium-high heat, cook the ground beef for about 5 minutes, crumbling with a spoon, until browned.

2 Add the onion and green bell pepper. Cook for about 5 minutes, stirring occasionally, until the vegetables are soft.

3 Add the garlic. Cook for 30 to 60 seconds, stirring constantly, until fragrant.

4 Add the black soybeans, crushed tomatoes, beef broth, chili powder, cayenne pepper, cumin, oregano, salt, and black pepper. Simmer for another 5 minutes, stirring occasionally.

5 Portion among 4 bowls, top each with 2 ounces of Monterey Jack cheese and one-quarter of the scallions, and serve.

TRY IT THIS WAY: For an even lower-carb version, eliminate the black soybeans altogether. It will save you about 11 grams of net carbohydrates.

CHILI COLORADO

SERVES 8 ▪ PREP TIME: 10 MINUTES ▪ COOK TIME: 8 HOURS, 15 MINUTES

2 dried New Mexico chiles

2 dried chipotle chiles

2 pounds pork shoulder, cut into 1-inch cubes

1 onion, chopped

4 garlic cloves, chopped

1 teaspoon ground cumin

½ teaspoon dried oregano

1 teaspoon salt

½ teaspoon freshly ground black pepper

1 cup unsalted beef broth

8 low-carb tortillas

16 ounces Monterey Jack cheese, grated, divided

1 cup sour cream, divided

1 cup salsa, divided

PER SERVING
Calories: 765; Total carbs: 19g;
Net carbs: 12g; Fiber: 7g; Fat: 55g;
Protein: 48g; Sodium: 1,391mg

Chili Colorado features chunks of tender pork braised all day in dried powdered chiles. The result is a tender, smoky, deeply satisfying dish. Many people like to put chili Colorado in a burrito. We do that here by adding cheese and a low-carb tortilla.

1 In a food processor fitted with a chopping blade, process the New Mexico chiles and chipotle chiles until ground into a powder.

2 In a slow cooker, stir together the pork, ground chiles, onion, garlic, cumin, oregano, salt, pepper, and beef broth to combine well. Cover and cook on low for 8 hours, or until the pork is tender.

3 Preheat the oven to 350°F.

4 Line a baking sheet with parchment paper, and place the tortillas on top.

5 Spoon equal amounts of chili onto each tortilla.

6 Add 2 ounces of Monterey Jack cheese to each, and roll the tortillas into burritos.

7 Bake for 15 minutes, or until the cheese melts and the tortillas brown.

8 Top with the sour cream and salsa, and serve.

TIMESAVING TIP: Waiting all day for chili Colorado to cook can be an awfully slow way to satisfy a craving. Try this if you just can't wait: Make the chili Colorado ahead of those cravings. Freeze it in individual portions in tightly sealed containers for up to six months.

JAMBALAYA

SERVES 4 ■ PREP TIME: 5 MINUTES ■ COOK TIME: 25 MINUTES

GF DF

1 head cauliflower, broken into florets

4 slices pepper bacon, cut into pieces

½ pound andouille sausage

½ onion, chopped

½ green bell pepper, chopped

1 celery stalk, chopped

3 garlic cloves, minced

2 tablespoons tomato paste

1 (14-ounce) can crushed tomatoes

1 cup unsalted chicken broth

½ pound medium shrimp, peeled, deveined, and tails removed

½ teaspoon salt

¼ teaspoon freshly ground black pepper

PER SERVING
Calories: 356; Total carbs: 18g; Net carbs: 12g; Fiber: 6g; Fat: 18g; Protein: 31g; Sodium: 1,455mg

This classic Creole dish combines savory and spicy andouille sausage with sweet shrimp and vegetables. The cauliflower rice soaks up all the flavors. Let the good times roll!

1 In a food processor fitted with a chopping blade, quickly pulse the cauliflower florets about 10 times, until they resemble rice.

2 In a large pot over medium-high heat, cook the bacon for about 5 minutes, or until it is browned and the fat has rendered. Using a slotted spoon, transfer the bacon from the pot to a paper towel–lined plate and set aside.

3 To the fat remaining in the pot, add the andouille sausage. Cook for about 6 minutes, stirring occasionally, until browned.

4 Add the onion, green bell pepper, and celery. Cook for about 5 minutes, stirring occasionally, until the vegetables are soft.

5 Add the garlic. Cook for 30 to 60 seconds, stirring constantly, until fragrant.

6 Add the tomato paste. Cook for 3 to 4 minutes, stirring constantly, until it begins to brown.

7 Stir in the crushed tomatoes and chicken broth, scraping any browned bits from the bottom of the pot. Bring to a simmer.

8 Stir in the shrimp, salt, pepper, and reserved cauliflower. Cook for about 5 minutes more, stirring frequently, until the shrimp is pink and the cauliflower softens, and serve.

WHY IT WORKS: Cajun cooking gets its flavor from roux, a mixture of flour and butter cooked until brown, plus the "holy trinity" of Cajun cooking—bell peppers, onions, and celery. Browning the tomato paste adds the complex flavors you get from browning a roux.

BEEF STEW

SERVES 4 ■ PREP TIME: 15 MINUTES ■ COOK TIME: 2 HOURS

GF DF

1 pound beef chuck roast,
    cut into 1-inch chunks
1 teaspoon sea salt
¼ teaspoon freshly ground
    black pepper
6 bacon slices, cut into pieces
1 onion, roughly chopped
3 large carrots, roughly chopped
2 celery stalks, chopped
1 pound cremini mushrooms,
    quartered
4 garlic cloves, chopped
1 cup dry red wine
1 cup unsalted beef broth
8 ounces frozen pearl onions
2 medium zucchini,
    cut into chunks
1 teaspoon dried thyme
¼ cup chopped fresh parsley

PER SERVING
Calories: 627; Total carbs: 25g;
Net carbs: 20g; Fiber: 5g; Fat: 26g;
Protein: 40g; Sodium: 1,488mg

A good beef stew takes time to cook, but the results are totally worth it. With a savory gravy, tender chunks of beef, and flavorful vegetables, beef stew is the perfect hearty dinner. This stew freezes well, so you can keep some on hand for the next craving crisis.

1 Preheat the oven to 325°F.

2 Season the beef with the sea salt and pepper. Set aside.

3 In a large ovenproof Dutch oven with a lid over medium-high heat, cook the bacon for about 5 minutes, or until brown and crispy. Using a slotted spoon, transfer the bacon from the pot to a platter and set aside.

4 To the fat remaining in the pot, add the seasoned beef. Cook for about 7 minutes, turning occasionally, until browned on all sides. Using tongs, remove the beef from the pot and set aside with the bacon.

5 To the fat remaining in the pot, add the onion, carrots, celery, and mushrooms. Cook for about 7 minutes, stirring occasionally, until the vegetables are soft and beginning to brown.

6 Add the garlic. Cook for 30 to 60 seconds, stirring constantly, until fragrant.

7 Stir in the red wine, scraping any browned bits from the bottom of the pot.

8 Stir in the beef broth.

9 Return the beef and bacon to the pot.

10 Add the pearl onions, zucchini, and thyme. Bring to a boil, stirring occasionally.

11 Cover the pot and transfer it to the preheated oven. Cook, covered, for about 90 minutes, or until the beef is tender. Remove from the oven.

12 Using tongs, remove the carrot chunks and place them in a food processor fitted with a chopping blade. Add ½ cup of the hot broth as well. Process for about 30 seconds, or until the carrots are puréed.

13 Return the carrot purée to the stew, stirring to thicken the stew slightly.

14 Stir in the parsley, and serve.

WHY IT WORKS: Traditionally, a fat and flour roux thickens beef stew, but it brings with it a lot of carbs. Here, the carrots are puréed to use as a thickener for the gravy. While potatoes are traditional to beef stew, zucchini replaces them here.

GOULASH

SERVES 4 ▪ PREP TIME: 20 MINUTES ▪ COOK TIME: 1 HOUR, 50 MINUTES

GF

- 4 tablespoons unsalted butter, divided
- 1 pound beef chuck roast, cut into 1-inch pieces
- ½ teaspoon salt
- ¼ teaspoon freshly ground black pepper
- 1 onion, chopped
- 1 garlic clove
- 2 tablespoons sweet paprika
- 1 cup unsalted beef broth
- 1 (14-ounce) can crushed tomatoes, undrained
- 3 zucchini
- 2 tablespoons sour cream

PER SERVING
Calories: 617; Total carbs: 18g;
Net carbs: 11g; Fiber: 7g; Fat: 45g;
Protein: 36g; Sodium: 691mg

Tender cuts of beef cooked in tasty sweet paprika melt in your mouth in this Hungarian goulash recipe. Traditionally, goulash is served on egg noodles or spaetzle. Here, zucchini ribbons fill in for the noodles, creating a satisfying yet flavorful low-carb meal.

1 Preheat the oven to 325°F.

2 In a large ovenproof Dutch oven with a lid over medium-high heat, melt 2 tablespoons of butter.

3 Season the beef with salt and pepper, and add it to the butter. Cook for 7 to 8 minutes, turning occasionally, until it is browned on all sides. Using tongs, transfer the beef to a plate and set aside.

4 Add the onion to the pot. Cook for about 5 minutes, stirring occasionally, until it begins to brown.

5 Add the garlic. Cook for 30 to 60 seconds, stirring constantly, until fragrant.

6 Stir in the sweet paprika, beef broth, and tomatoes, scraping any browned bits from the bottom of the pot.

7 Return the reserved beef to the pot. Bring to a simmer.

8 Cover the pot, and place it in the preheated oven. Cook for about 90 minutes, or until the beef is tender.

9 While the beef cooks, using a vegetable peeler, cut the zucchini into long ribbons. Cut the ribbons into halves or thirds, crosswise.

10 When the beef is tender, remove the pot from the oven.

11 Stir in the sour cream.

12 In a large nonstick skillet over medium-high heat, heat the remaining 2 tablespoons of butter.

13 Add the zucchini. Cook for about 4 minutes, stirring occasionally, until soft.

14 Spoon the goulash over the zucchini noodles and serve.

SANDWICHES, WRAPS, AND MORE

GRILLED CHEESE

SERVES 2 ▪ PREP TIME: 15 MINUTES, PLUS 30 MINUTES TO DRAIN ▪
COOK TIME: 35 MINUTES, PLUS 10 MINUTES COOLING TIME

GF V

FOR THE CAULIFLOWER BREAD
Cooking spray
1 head cauliflower, cut into florets
1 tablespoon unsalted butter
1 large egg, beaten
½ teaspoon garlic powder
½ teaspoon onion powder
½ teaspoon salt
¼ teaspoon freshly ground
   black pepper
2 ounces grated Parmesan cheese

FOR THE SANDWICHES
2 tablespoons unsalted butter,
   melted, divided
4 ounces Cheddar cheese,
   grated, divided

PER SERVING
Calories: 491; Total carbs: 10g;
Net carbs: 6g; Fiber: 4g; Fat: 39g;
Protein: 30g; Sodium: 1,350mg

Grilled cheese sandwiches are the ultimate crave-creating food. With gooey cheese melted between crispy, buttery slices of bread, they're simple, delicious, and delightful. While this carb-friendly version takes a bit more time and effort, the end result is perfect for when nothing but a grilled cheese sandwich will do.

TO MAKE THE CAULIFLOWER BREAD

1 Preheat the oven to 450°F.

2 Line a baking sheet with parchment paper, and coat with cooking spray.

3 In a food processor fitted with a chopping blade, quickly pulse the cauliflower about 15 times, or until it resembles rice.

4 In a large skillet over medium-high heat, heat the butter. Add the cauliflower. Cook for about 10 minutes, stirring occasionally, until soft.

5 Transfer the cauliflower to a fine-mesh sieve, and hold it over the sink. Using the back of a wooden spoon, press out all the excess moisture you can. If you want to be very thorough, put the sieve over a bowl. Place a small plate on top of the cauliflower, and add a weight, like a large can of tomatoes, on top. Let it sit for 30 minutes. Then, press the cauliflower again with the spoon to make sure all the moisture is out.

6 In a large bowl, mix together the cauliflower, egg, garlic powder, onion powder, salt, pepper, and Parmesan cheese.

7 On the prepared baking sheet, divide the mixture into 4 equal mounds. Shape each into a bread-slice shape.

8 Bake for 15 to 17 minutes, or until golden brown. Remove from the oven, and cool for 10 minutes. Remove from the baking sheet.

1 Heat a nonstick skillet over medium-high heat.

2 Brush one side of each of the 4 cauliflower bread slices with 1½ teaspoons of melted butter. Place 2 slices, butter-side down, in the skillet.

3 Spread 2 ounces of Cheddar cheese evenly on each slice. Top each with 1 of the remaining slices of bread, butter-side up.

4 Cook for about 3 minutes, or until browned. Flip. Cook for 3 minutes more on the other side until browned, and serve.

WHY IT WORKS: Drying the cauliflower by squeezing out all the excess moisture is the most important step in this process. It allows the bread to hold together firmly, giving you the perfect base for your grilled cheese.

BEEF, CHEESE, AND CARAMELIZED ONION PANINI

SERVES 2 ▪ PREP TIME: 10 MINUTES ▪ COOK TIME: 40 MINUTES

GF

FOR THE CARAMELIZED ONIONS

2 tablespoons unsalted butter

½ onion, sliced

¼ teaspoon salt

¼ teaspoon dried thyme

FOR THE SANDWICH

1 recipe Cauliflower Bread
   (page 90)

2 tablespoons unsalted butter,
   melted, divided

4 ounces Swiss cheese,
   grated, divided

4 (1-ounce) deli roast beef slices

PER SERVING
Calories: 764; Total carbs: 15g;
Net carbs: 11g; Fiber: 4g; Fat: 62g;
Protein: 41g; Sodium: 2,068mg

This recipe follows the same method as the Grilled Cheese sandwich (page 90). Loaded with sweet and savory caramelized onions, roast beef, and Swiss cheese, it's the perfect grilled reduced-carb sandwich to satisfy your craving.

TO MAKE THE CARAMELIZED ONIONS

1 In a medium skillet over medium-low heat, heat the butter.

2 Add the onions, salt, and thyme. Cook for about 30 minutes, stirring occasionally, until the onions are browned and caramelized.

TO MAKE THE SANDWICH

1 Preheat a large skillet over medium-high heat.

2 Brush one side of each of 4 Cauliflower Bread slices with 1½ teaspoons of melted butter.

3 Place 2 slices, butter-side down, in the skillet.

4 Top each with 2 ounces of Swiss cheese, 2 slices of roast beef, and half of the caramelized onions.

5 Top each with 1 of the remaining slices of bread, butter-side up.

6 Cook for about 3 minutes, or until browned. Flip. Cook for 3 minutes more on the other side, until browned, and serve.

TIMESAVING TIP: Caramelized onions freeze perfectly. Cook a big batch, and freeze them in single servings in a tightly sealed container for up to one year. Then thaw as you need them.

FRENCH DIP

SERVES 2 ▪ PREP TIME: 10 MINUTES ▪ COOK TIME: 5 MINUTES

2 tablespoons unsalted
 butter, melted

½ teaspoon garlic powder

1 recipe Cauliflower Bread
 (page 90)

6 (1-ounce) deli roast beef slices

1 package au jus gravy mix

2 cups water

PER SERVING
Calories: 478; Total carbs: 11g;
Net carbs: 7g; Fiber: 4g; Fat: 36g;
Protein: 30g; Sodium: 2,346mg

There's just something about roast beef sandwiches dipped in warm au jus that is delicious and craveable. Serve this sandwich with a side of Onion Rings (page 66) or French Fries (page 65) for a classic pub-style meal.

1 Preheat the broiler.

2 In a small bowl, mix together the butter and garlic powder.

3 Spread both sides of the Cauliflower Bread slices with equal amounts of the garlic butter. Place on a baking sheet and place the sheet under the broiler. Toast the bread for 1 to 2 minutes per side, or until golden on both sides, watching carefully so it doesn't burn. Remove from the oven.

4 Lay out 2 pieces of bread. Top each with 3 slices of roast beef. Place 1 of the remaining bread slices atop each. Cut each sandwich in half.

5 In a small saucepan over high heat, stir together the au jus mix and water. Bring to a boil, whisking occasionally. Divide between 2 bowls.

6 Serve the sandwiches with the au jus for dipping.

TACOS

SERVES 4 ▪ PREP TIME: 10 MINUTES ▪ COOK TIME: 25 MINUTES

GF

8 slices provolone cheese

½ pound ground beef

½ onion, finely chopped

3 garlic cloves, minced

¼ cup water

1 tablespoon chili powder

1 teaspoon ground cumin

1 teaspoon dried oregano

½ teaspoon salt

¼ teaspoon freshly ground
    black pepper

1 cup shredded lettuce

1 tomato, chopped

4 scallions, chopped

½ cup sour cream

2 ounces Cheddar cheese, grated

¼ cup salsa

PER SERVING
Calories: 453; Total carbs: 9g;
Net carbs: 7g; Fiber: 2g; Fat: 30g;
Protein: 38g; Sodium: 1,045mg

Have a hankering for savory, spicy tacos in a crispy, crunchy shell? These carb-friendly tacos have all the spicy flavors in the meat and fillings, and they're served in a crispy cheese shell with a satisfying crunch.

1 Preheat the oven to 375°F.

2 Line a baking sheet with parchment paper. Cut 4 additional parchment squares, each large enough to accommodate 2 slices of provolone cheese.

3 On each parchment square, place 2 slices of provolone cheese, side by side and overlapping slightly. Place the squares on the prepared baking sheet.

4 Bake for about 10 minutes, or until golden brown.

5 Remove from the oven and immediately lift each cheese shell by the parchment squares. Drape them over the edge of a deep, rimmed pan, such as a bread pan, parchment-side down. The cheese will crisp and cool in the shape of a taco shell.

6 In a large skillet over medium-high heat, add the ground beef. Cook for 5 to 7 minutes, crumbling with a spoon, until browned.

7 Add the onion. Cook for about 4 minutes more, stirring occasionally, until soft.

8 Add the garlic. Cook for 30 to 60 seconds, stirring constantly, until fragrant.

9 Stir in the water, chili powder, cumin, oregano, salt, and pepper. Cook for about 3 minutes more, stirring constantly, until the seasonings coat the meat.

10 To assemble the tacos, spoon the ground beef into the shells. Top each taco with one-quarter each of the lettuce, tomato, scallions, sour cream, cheese, and salsa, and serve.

STEAK FAJITAS

SERVES 4 ▪ PREP TIME: 10 MINUTES, PLUS 4 HOURS TO MARINATE ▪ COOK TIME: 20 MINUTES

¼ cup freshly squeezed
  lime juice

½ cup fresh cilantro

6 scallions, chopped

3 garlic cloves, chopped

1 jalapeño pepper, seeded and
  chopped

¼ cup plus 2 tablespoons extra-
  virgin olive oil, divided

1 teaspoon salt

½ teaspoon freshly ground
  black pepper

1 pound beef flank steak,
  or tri-tip steak

½ green bell pepper, thinly sliced

½ onion, thinly sliced

4 low-carb tortillas

1 recipe Guacamole (page 60)

¼ cup sour cream

4 ounces Monterey Jack
  cheese, grated

PER SERVING
Calories: 791; Total carbs: 21g;
Net carbs: 13g; Fiber: 8g; Fat: 63g;
Protein: 40g; Sodium: 1,797mg

Sizzling fajitas inspire cravings because of their savory beef flavor combined with Latin spices and the sweetness of the onions and peppers. To make them low carb, simply replace the regular tortillas with low-carb tortillas.

1 In a food processor fitted with a chopping blade, combine the lime juice, cilantro, scallions, garlic, jalapeño, ¼ cup of olive oil, the salt, and pepper. Process until well combined.

2 Put all but 2 tablespoons of the marinade in a large resealable bag. Set aside the 2 tablespoons of marinade.

3 Add the steak to the bag, turning to coat well. Refrigerate for at least 4 hours to marinate.

4 Remove the steak from the marinade. Using a paper towel, wipe away any excess marinade from the meat's surface.

5 In a large skillet (cast iron works well) over medium-high heat, heat the remaining 2 tablespoons of olive oil until it shimmers.

6 Add the steak. Cook for 3 to 4 minutes per side, or until deeply browned on both sides. Transfer the steak to a platter or cutting board. Tent with aluminum foil to keep warm and to rest.

7 To the skillet, add the green bell pepper and onion. Cook for 6 to 7 minutes, stirring occasionally, or until the vegetables begin to brown.

8 Slice the steak across the grain into thin strips. Add the strips to the hot skillet with the peppers and onions.

9 Add the reserved 2 tablespoons of marinade. Cook for 1 to 2 minutes, or until the vegetables and meat are coated with the marinade.

10 Spoon the mixture evenly into the tortillas, and serve with the Guacamole, sour cream, and Monterey Jack cheese.

CHICKEN AND CHEESE BURRITOS

SERVES 4 ▪ PREP TIME: 10 MINUTES, PLUS 2 HOURS TO MARINATE ▪ COOK TIME: 35 MINUTES

Burritos are another frequently craved southwestern favorite. With melted cheese, refried beans, and seasoned meat, they offer a perfect balance of spicy and cooling ingredients. They are also a convenient grab-and-go food, thanks to their convenient self-contained wrapper. This burrito meets all those criteria, and your lower-carb needs, too.

FOR THE CHICKEN

- 8 ounces boneless, skinless chicken thighs, cut into bite-size pieces
- ½ cup extra-virgin olive oil
- ¼ cup freshly squeezed lime juice
- 1 teaspoon garlic powder
- 1 teaspoon chili powder
- 1 teaspoon onion powder
- ½ teaspoon ground cumin
- ⅛ teaspoon cayenne pepper
- ½ teaspoon salt
- 2 tablespoons unsalted butter

FOR THE BEANS

- 1 cup black soybeans, undrained
- ¼ cup salsa
- ¼ teaspoon ground cumin
- ¼ teaspoon salt
- 3 ounces pepper Jack cheese, grated

FOR THE BURRITOS

- 4 low-carb tortillas
- 4 ounces pepper Jack cheese, grated

PER SERVING
Calories: 933; Total carbs: 30g; Net carbs: 19g; Fiber: 11g; Fat: 68g; Protein: 53g; Sodium: 1,428mg

TO MAKE THE CHICKEN

1 Put the chicken in a large resealable plastic bag.

2 In a small bowl, whisk together the olive oil, lime juice, garlic powder, chili powder, onion powder, cumin, cayenne pepper, and salt. Pour it into the bag with the chicken. Refrigerate for 2 hours to marinate.

3 In a large skillet over medium-high heat, heat the butter.

4 Remove the chicken from the marinade, and add it to the skillet. Cook for 5 to 7 minutes, stirring occasionally, until cooked through.

TO MAKE THE BEANS

1 In a medium saucepan over medium heat, stir together the black soybeans, salsa, cumin, and salt. Cook for about 5 minutes, stirring occasionally, until heated through.

2 Using a potato masher, mash the beans.

3 Stir in the cheese until it melts.

1 Preheat the oven to 350°F.

2 Spread each tortilla with one-quarter of the soybean mixture. Top each with one-quarter of the chicken and 1 ounce of pepper Jack cheese.

3 Roll the tortillas around the filling, tucking in the ends. Place them on a baking sheet seam-side down.

4 Bake for about 20 minutes, or until the filling warms and the cheese melts, and serve.

TIMESAVING TIP: Save time by using a rotisserie chicken. Simply shred the meat and toss it with a cup of your favorite salsa.

PHILLY CHEESESTEAK

SERVES 4 ▪ PREP TIME: 10 MINUTES ▪ COOK TIME: 1 HOUR, 10 MINUTES

GF

- 4 green bell peppers, tops removed, seeded
- 4 tablespoons unsalted butter, divided
- 1 pound strip loin steak, or tri-tip steak, cut across the grain into thin strips
- ½ teaspoon salt
- ¼ teaspoon freshly ground black pepper
- 8 ounces button mushrooms, sliced
- 1 recipe Caramelized Onions (page 92)
- 4 ounces provolone cheese, grated
- 4 ounces Parmesan cheese, grated

PER SERVING
Calories: 596; Total carbs: 10g; Net carbs: 7g; Fiber: 3g; Fat: 38g; Protein: 54g; Sodium: 1,007mg

This Philadelphia masterpiece has become known world-wide for its combination of gooey provolone cheese, savory caramelized onions, sautéed peppers and mushrooms, and its chewy and flavorful steak. It's a savory and salty treat with bold flavors that you just need to have now—and you can, when you make this delicious alternative to the traditional carb-loaded version.

1 Preheat the oven to 350°F.

2 In a 9-inch square baking dish, place the bell peppers cut-side up.

3 In a large skillet over medium-high heat, heat 2 tablespoons of butter.

4 Season the steak with salt and pepper. Add it to the skillet. Cook for about 2 minutes per side, or until cooked through.

5 Using tongs, transfer the steak to a large bowl and set aside.

6 Add the remaining 2 tablespoons of butter to the skillet.

7 Add the mushrooms. Cook for about 7 minutes, stirring occasionally, until browned.

8 Transfer the mushrooms to the bowl with the beef.

9 Stir in the Caramelized Onions, provolone cheese, and Parmesan cheese.

10 Fill the bell peppers with equal amounts of the steak mixture, and cover with aluminum foil.

11 Bake for about 1 hour, or until the peppers are tender, and serve.

WHY IT WORKS: The bread itself really doesn't add much flavor to the cheesesteak sandwich; it just serves as a receptacle. Here, you have all the fantastic flavors, but they are stuffed in a green bell pepper, making the bread unnecessary.

CORN DOGS

SERVES 4 ■ PREP TIME: 5 MINUTES ■ COOK TIME: 15 MINUTES

GF DF

Coconut oil, for frying
1 cup almond flour
1¼ teaspoons baking powder
½ packet stevia
¼ teaspoon garlic powder
¼ teaspoon salt
2 large eggs
1 large egg yolk
4 sugar-free frankfurters

PER SERVING
Calories: 307; Total carbs: 5g;
Net carbs: 4g; Fiber: 1g; Fat: 28g;
Protein: 10g; Sodium: 574mg

Remember when you were a kid at a carnival with a corn dog? Nothing tasted better than that salty dog surrounded by the slightly sweet and crispy fried cornmeal dough. Fortunately, these corn dogs aren't off limits for low-carbers, but hold the cotton candy!

1 In a large pot over medium-high, heat 2 inches of coconut oil until it reaches 350°F on a candy thermometer.

2 In a medium bowl, whisk together the almond flour, baking powder, stevia, garlic powder, and salt.

3 In a small bowl, whisk together the eggs and egg yolk.

4 Add the eggs to the almond flour mixture, whisking until well combined.

5 Using a paper towel, blot any moisture from the surface of the frankfurters. Thread a wooden skewer through the bottom of each.

6 Working one at a time, holding the stick, dip the frankfurter into the batter, coating it entirely and allowing any excess to drip away. Immediately put the battered frankfurter into the hot coconut oil.

7 Cook for about 2 minutes, or until golden brown. Turn the corn dog over. Cook for 2 to 3 minutes more on the other side, until browned. Repeat with the other frankfurters.

8 Drain the frankfurters on paper towels.

9 Cool slightly and serve.

CHILI DOGS

SERVES 4 ■ PREP TIME: 5 MINUTES ■ COOK TIME: 10 MINUTES

GF

1 recipe Chili Con Carne
    (page 81)
2 tablespoons unsalted butter
4 sugar-free frankfurters, sliced
4 ounces Cheddar cheese, grated

PER SERVING
Calories: 749; Total carbs: 33g;
Net carbs: 23g; Fiber: 10g; Fat: 46g;
Protein: 52g; Sodium: 1,476mg

Chili dogs seem sinful—with two kinds of meat (ground beef and a hot dog) sharing the same bun. They are also delicious. The salty hot dog just seems to have an affinity for the chili. This recipe uses Chili Con Carne (page 81) for a tasty treat, minus the sinfulness.

1 In a large saucepan over medium heat, cook the Chili Con Carne for about 5 minutes, stirring occasionally, until warm.

2 In a large skillet over medium-high heat, heat the butter.

3 Add the sliced frankfurters. Cook for about 5 minutes, stirring occasionally, until browned.

4 Stir the cooked franks into the chili.

5 Portion the chili into 4 bowls. Top each bowl with 1 ounce of Cheddar cheese, and serve.

WHY IT WORKS: With a traditional chili dog, the bun gets lost beneath all the chili, so it doesn't add any flavor. Likewise, you typically eat chili dogs with a fork or spoon. This version eliminates the bun altogether, giving you the flavors without the carbs.

PULLED PORK

SERVES 4 ▪ PREP TIME: 15 MINUTES ▪ COOK TIME: 8 HOURS

DF

FOR THE PULLED PORK

1 pound pork shoulder, or boneless country-style pork ribs

1½ cups Barbecue Sauce (page 168)

FOR THE COLESLAW

¼ cup mayonnaise

2 tablespoons apple cider vinegar

½ teaspoon salt

1 cup shredded cabbage

2 carrots, grated

FOR THE WRAP

4 low-carb tortillas

PER SERVING
Calories: 569; Total carbs: 26g;
Net carbs: 17g; Fiber: 9g; Fat: 36g;
Protein: 34g; Sodium: 1,468mg

With sweet and smoky barbecue sauce and savory fatty pork, pulled pork is a delicious and flavorful sandwich filling. Adding coleslaw gives the sandwich a crispy texture. In this case, instead of a high-carb bun, a low-carb tortilla is used, making it a wrap sandwich.

TO MAKE THE PULLED PORK

1 In a slow cooker, combine the pork and Barbecue Sauce.

2 Cover and cook on low for 8 hours.

3 Remove the pork from the slow cooker. Using two forks, shred the pork by pulling the forks in opposite directions.

4 Return the shredded pork to the slow cooker. Stir to coat with the Barbecue Sauce. Set aside.

TO MAKE THE COLESLAW

1 In a small bowl, whisk together the mayonnaise, apple cider vinegar, and salt.

2 In a large bowl, toss the cabbage and carrots with the dressing.

TO MAKE THE WRAP

1 Spoon the pulled pork onto the tortillas.

2 Top with the coleslaw.

3 Wrap the tortillas around the filling, and serve.

TRY IT THIS WAY: If you don't have a slow cooker, put the ingredients for the pulled pork in a large Dutch oven. Cover and bring to a simmer on the stove top. Then transfer the pot to a 325°F oven and cook for about 4 hours.

BACON CHEESEBURGERS

SERVES 4 ▪ PREP TIME: 15 MINUTES ▪ COOK TIME: 1 HOUR, 5 MINUTES

FOR THE BUNS

3 large eggs, separated

⅛ teaspoon cream of tartar

¼ teaspoon stevia

⅛ teaspoon salt

¼ teaspoon garlic powder

¼ teaspoon onion powder

3 ounces cream cheese,
    at room temperature

FOR THE BURGER SAUCE

½ cup mayonnaise

¼ teaspoon stevia

1 garlic clove, minced

1 tablespoon
    Worcestershire sauce

1 tablespoon soy sauce

¼ teaspoon sriracha

FOR THE BURGER

1 pound ground beef

1 teaspoon salt

¼ teaspoon freshly ground
    black pepper

1 tablespoon
    Worcestershire sauce

4 slices Swiss cheese

8 crisply cooked bacon
    slices, halved

4 tomato slices

4 lettuce leaves

4 thin slices red onion

PER SERVING
Calories: 625; Total carbs: 14g;
Net carbs: 14g; Fiber: 0g; Fat: 39g;
Protein: 52g; Sodium: 1,559mg

Sometimes, you just want a big, greasy cheeseburger. In the low-carb world, satisfying this craving often means staring at a sad, naked hamburger patty. Fortunately, that doesn't need to happen here. These rolls give you something to hold onto, so you can eat your burger with all of the fixings in a tasty bun.

TO MAKE THE BUNS

1 Preheat the oven to 300°F.

2 Line a baking sheet with parchment paper.

3 In a large bowl, using a hand-held mixer or whisk, whip together the egg whites and cream of tartar until stiff.

4 In a small bowl, using a hand-held mixer with clean beaters, beat together the egg yolks, stevia, salt, garlic powder, onion powder, and cream cheese until well blended.

5 Gently fold the cream cheese mixture into the egg whites until just blended.

6 Spoon the mixture onto the prepared baking sheet in 4 equal-size mounds. Bake for 30 minutes.

7 Remove from the oven. Cool the buns on the sheet for about 5 minutes. Transfer them to a wire rack to cool completely.

8 Using a serrated knife, gently cut the cooled buns in half crosswise.

TO MAKE THE BURGER SAUCE

In a small bowl, whisk together the mayonnaise, stevia, garlic, Worcestershire sauce, soy sauce, and sriracha. Set aside.

1 Preheat the oven to 400°F.

2 Place a baking rack on a rimmed baking sheet.

3 In a large bowl, mix together the ground beef, salt, pepper, and Worcestershire sauce until well blended.

4 Form the mixture into 4 patties, and put them on the prepared baking sheet.

5 Bake for 20 to 30 minutes, or until they reach an internal temperature of 145°F on an instant-read thermometer. Turn off the oven.

6 Top each burger with 1 slice of Swiss cheese. Close the oven door. Leave the burgers in the turned-off oven for about 3 minutes, or until the cheese melts.

7 Spread the split buns with the burger sauce. Top the bottom half of each bun with 1 beef patty, 2 pieces of bacon, 1 tomato slice, 1 lettuce leaf, 1 red onion slice. and the top bun half before devouring.

WHY IT WORKS: The air pumped into the egg whites during beating is what holds the buns together. Therefore, it is very important to fold in the egg yolk mixture carefully so you don't collapse the bun. Cooling the buns before cutting helps maintain their structural integrity.

GYROS

SERVES 4 ■ PREP TIME: 15 MINUTES, PLUS 1 HOUR TO MARINATE ■
COOK TIME: 1 HOUR, PLUS 20 MINUTES RESTING TIME

FOR THE PICKLED RED ONIONS

½ cup red wine vinegar

½ packet stevia

1 teaspoon salt

½ red onion, thinly sliced

FOR THE GYRO MEAT

½ onion, cut into chunks

6 garlic cloves, chopped

2 tablespoons chopped
    fresh rosemary

1 tablespoon chopped
    fresh oregano

1 teaspoon salt

½ teaspoon freshly ground
    black pepper

1 pound ground lamb

FOR THE GARLIC MAYONNAISE

½ cup mayonnaise

2 garlic cloves, finely minced

Pinch salt

1 tablespoon freshly squeezed
    lemon juice

FOR THE WRAPS

4 low-carb tortillas

4 ounces crumbled feta cheese

1 tomato, chopped

1 cucumber, chopped

2 cups baby arugula

PER SERVING
Calories: 594; Total carbs: 32g;
Net carbs: 23g; Fiber: 9g; Fat: 32g;
Protein: 44g; Sodium: 2,275mg

Gyros have savory Mediterranean flavors that blend beautifully with ground lamb. When combined with spicy, garlicky mayonnaise, pickled red onions, salty feta cheese, sweet tomatoes, and peppery arugula, the combination of flavors makes your taste buds do a happy dance. Even more reason to dance—this version doesn't break your carb bank!

TO MAKE THE PICKLED RED ONIONS

1 In a small bowl, whisk together the red wine vinegar, stevia, and salt until the salt dissolves.

2 Add the red onions. Allow to sit for 1 hour.

TO MAKE THE GYRO MEAT

1 Preheat the oven to 325°F.

2 Place a 9-by-13-inch baking dish in the oven. Carefully fill it one-third full with boiling water to create a water bath.

3 In a food processor fitted with a chopping blade, process the onion and garlic for about 1 minute, or until it is completely chopped.

4 Transfer the mixture to a clean kitchen towel. Wrap it completely around the onions and garlic. Over the sink, twist the towel to squeeze the water completely out of the onions.

5 Using a paper towel, wipe any excess moisture out of the food processor. Return the onions to the processor.

6 Add the rosemary, oregano, salt, pepper, and lamb. Process for 2 to 3 minutes, or until all the ingredients combine and form a paste, pausing to scrape down the sides if necessary.

7 Transfer the mixture to a small loaf pan, and spread it out. Put the loaf pan in the water bath. Bake for about 1 hour, or until the gyro meat reaches 145°F on an instant-read thermometer.

8 Remove from the oven and allow to rest for 20 minutes before slicing.

9 Cut the gyro meat into thin slices.

TO MAKE THE GARLIC MAYONNAISE

In a small bowl, whisk together the mayonnaise, garlic, salt, and lemon juice.

TO MAKE THE WRAPS

1 Evenly divide the gyro slices among the 4 tortillas. Top each with one-quarter of the pickled onions, 1 tablespoon of garlic mayonnaise, 1 ounce of feta cheese, one-quarter of the chopped tomato, one-quarter of the cucumber, and ½ cup of arugula.

2 Wrap the tortillas around the filling, and serve.

PIZZAS AND PASTAS

BASIC PIZZA CRUST

MAKES 1 CRUST ▪ PREP TIME: 10 MINUTES ▪ COOK TIME: 30 MINUTES, PLUS 30 MINUTES DRAINING TIME

GF V

½ head cauliflower, cut into florets
1 egg, beaten
1¼ cups grated mozzarella cheese
¼ cup grated Parmesan cheese
½ teaspoon garlic powder
¼ teaspoon onion powder
½ teaspoon dried oregano
½ teaspoon salt

PER SERVING (¼ crust)
Calories: 170; Total carbs: 4g;
Net carbs: 3g; Fiber: 1g; Fat: 11g;
Protein: 17g; Sodium: 660mg

Many low-carbers really miss pizza. While you can take pizza toppings and make them into a casserole, sometimes you just really want a piece of pizza with a crust. This simple cauliflower crust makes it easy for you to create a small round crust for your low-carb pizza.

1 Preheat the oven to 375°F.

2 Line a baking sheet with parchment paper.

3 In a food processor fitted with a chopping blade, quickly pulse the cauliflower about 20 times, or until finely ground.

4 Spread the cauliflower on the prepared baking sheet, and roast for 15 minutes.

5 Remove from the oven. Transfer to a fine-mesh sieve and cover with a plate that fits inside the strainer. Put a weight, such as a large can of tomatoes, on the plate. Place the sieve over a bowl. Let sit for 30 minutes to drain off any remaining water.

6 Remove the weight and the plate. Press the cauliflower with a spoon to remove any remaining water. Alternatively, squeeze the cauliflower in a clean kitchen towel to wring out any remaining water.

7 Increase the oven temperature to 450°F.

8 In a large bowl, mix together the cauliflower, egg, mozzarella cheese, Parmesan cheese, garlic powder, onion powder, oregano, and salt.

9 Reline the baking sheet, or line a pizza pan, with parchment. Spread the cauliflower mixture evenly over the parchment paper. Bake for about 12 minutes, or until it begins to crisp.

10 Use the crust to make one of the delicious low-carb pizza recipes found in this chapter.

TRY IT THIS WAY: If you don't have a food processor, grate the cauliflower on a box grater for similar results.

MARGHERITA PIZZA

SERVES 4 ▪ PREP TIME: 10 MINUTES ▪ COOK TIME: 10 MINUTES

GF V

1 cooked Basic Pizza Crust
(page 108)

1 cup Marinara (page 67)

1 cup fresh basil leaves

8 ounces fresh mozzarella
cheese, sliced

PER SERVING
Calories: 387; Total carbs: 14g;
Net carbs: 11g; Fiber: 3g; Fat: 22g;
Protein: 34g; Sodium: 1,261mg

This fresh-tasting pizza delivers delicious Italian flavors and is gooey with fresh mozzarella cheese. You can find fresh mozzarella in the deli section of the grocery store. It has a much creamier consistency than packaged mozzarella. Indulge your cravings with this made-over version, and you'll say, "That's *amore!*"

1 Preheat the oven to 425°F.

2 Line a baking sheet, or pizza pan, with parchment paper.

3 Put the Basic Pizza Crust on the prepared sheet.

4 Spread the Marinara evenly over the crust.

5 Top with the basil leaves.

6 Scatter the mozzarella slices over the top.

7 Bake for about 10 minutes, or until the cheese is brown and melted.

8 Slice and serve.

VEGETARIAN PIZZA

SERVES 4 ▪ PREP TIME: 15 MINUTES ▪ COOK TIME: 15 MINUTES

GF V

1 cooked Basic Pizza Crust
  (page 108)

1 cup Alfredo Sauce (page 117)

1 cup baby spinach leaves

4 ounces button
  mushrooms, sliced

½ red onion, chopped

½ red bell pepper, chopped

½ green bell pepper, chopped

4 ounces mozzarella
  cheese, grated

2 ounces Parmesan cheese, grated

PER SERVING
Calories: 546; Total carbs: 10g;
Net carbs: 8g; Fiber: 2g; Fat: 43g;
Protein: 33g; Sodium: 1,143mg

If you like your pizza with a white sauce and full of fresh veggies, then this is the pizza for you. The cheesy white sauce makes the pizza decadently rich, while the fresh vegetables add flavor and fiber. No need for delivery when you can make this carb-friendly version so easily at home.

1 Preheat the oven to 425°F.

2 Line a baking sheet, or pizza pan, with parchment paper.

3 Put the Basic Pizza Crust on the prepared sheet.

4 Spread the Alfredo Sauce evenly over the crust.

5 Cover the pizza with the spinach.

6 Arrange the mushrooms, red onion, red bell pepper, and green bell pepper over the spinach.

7 In a small bowl, toss together the mozzarella cheese and Parmesan cheese. Sprinkle over the pizza.

8 Bake for about 15 minutes, or until the cheese melts and the vegetables soften.

9 Slice and serve.

MEAT LOVER'S PIZZA

SERVES 4 ▪ PREP TIME: 20 MINUTES ▪ COOK TIME: 25 MINUTES

GF

1 cooked Basic Pizza Crust
  (page 108)

1 cup Marinara (page 67)

½ pound bulk Italian sausage

4 ounces sliced pepperoni

4 ounces sliced salami

4 ounces sliced Canadian bacon

4 ounces mozzarella
  cheese, grated

2 ounces Parmesan
  cheese, grated

PER SERVING
Calories: 831; Total carbs: 14g;
Net carbs: 11g; Fiber: 3g; Fat: 60g;
Protein: 58g; Sodium: 3,001mg

If super meaty pizza is your thing, then this one will satisfy your craving. Full of hearty, meaty toppings like Italian sausage, pepperoni, and Canadian bacon, it's the perfect pizza for the dedicated carnivore living a low-carb lifestyle.

1 Preheat the oven to 425°F.

2 Line a baking sheet, or pizza pan, with parchment paper.

3 Put the Basic Pizza Crust on the sheet.

4 Spread the Marinara evenly over the crust.

5 In a large skillet over medium-high heat, cook the Italian sausage for 5 to 7 minutes, crumbing with a spoon, until it browns.

6 Distribute the sausage, pepperoni, salami, and Canadian bacon evenly over the pizza.

7 In a small bowl, toss together the mozzarella cheese and Parmesan cheese. Sprinkle over the pizza.

8 Bake for 10 to 15 minutes, or until the cheese melts.

9 Slice and serve.

PASTA PRIMAVERA

SERVES 4 ▪ PREP TIME: 20 MINUTES ▪ COOK TIME: 25 MINUTES

GF V

4 zucchini

Salt

4 tablespoons extra-virgin olive oil, divided

2 carrots, sliced

1 onion, chopped

1 red bell pepper, seeded and cut into strips

4 garlic cloves, minced

4 ounces mushrooms, sliced

¼ cup dry white wine (optional)

½ cup unsalted vegetable broth; increase to ¾ cup if omitting the white wine

½ cup heavy (whipping) cream

½ cup Asiago cheese, grated

¼ teaspoon freshly ground black pepper

¼ cup chopped fresh basil

PER SERVING
Calories: 391; Total carbs: 17g;
Net carbs: 12g; Fiber: 5g; Fat: 30g;
Protein: 14g; Sodium: 616mg

If pasta is tempting you, try this light dish filled with fresh vegetables. Savory mushrooms and salty cheese combine with the fresh vegetable flavors, making for a delicious plate of food. Of course, traditional pasta is very high in carbs, so make these few adjustments, and enjoy this fresh-tasting pasta anytime.

1 Using a vegetable peeler, cut the zucchini into thin ribbons. Cut the ribbons in half crosswise.

2 To a colander set over the sink or a bowl, add the zucchini. Sprinkle it with salt. Let it sit as you prepare the remaining ingredients so the salt can draw out the water.

3 In a large skillet over medium-high heat, heat 2 tablespoons of olive oil until it shimmers.

4 Add the carrots, onion, and red bell pepper. Cook for about 6 minutes, or until the vegetables are soft.

5 Add the garlic. Cook for about 30 to 60 seconds, stirring constantly, until fragrant.

6 Transfer the vegetables to a platter and set aside.

7 Return the skillet to the heat. Add the remaining 2 tablespoons of olive oil.

8 Add the mushrooms to the skillet. Cook for about 7 minutes, stirring occasionally, until they begin to brown.

9 Using a paper towel, wipe the salt and any moisture away from the zucchini. Add the zucchini to the skillet with the mushrooms. Cook for 2 minutes, stirring occasionally. Remove the vegetables from the skillet and set aside.

10 Stir in the white wine (if using), scraping any browned bits from the bottom of the skillet. If omitting the white wine, deglaze the pan in this step with ¼ cup of vegetable broth, and add the remaining ½ cup of broth in the next step. ►►

11 Stir in the vegetable broth and heavy cream. Stirring constantly, bring to a simmer.

12 Return the vegetables to the skillet. Cook for 2 to 3 minutes, stirring constantly, until warmed through.

13 Stir in the Asiago cheese and pepper. Cook for 3 minutes more, stirring constantly, until the cheese melts.

14 Stir in the basil, and serve.

WHY IT WORKS: Since pasta primavera already calls for zucchini, replacing the noodles with zucchini strips doesn't alter the flavor at all. Instead, you get all the flavor profile of the original without the carbs.

SHRIMP SCAMPI WITH SPAGHETTI

SERVES 4 ▪ PREP TIME: 10 MINUTES ▪ COOK TIME: 15 MINUTES

GF

4 zucchini

¼ cup extra-virgin olive oil

1 shallot, minced

1 pound medium shrimp, peeled, deveined, and tails removed

5 garlic cloves, minced

Juice of 1 lemon

Zest of ½ lemon

¼ cup dry white wine (optional)

½ teaspoon salt

¼ teaspoon freshly ground black pepper

1 cup unsalted chicken broth; increase to 1¼ cups if omitting the white wine

¼ cup chopped fresh Italian parsley

4 ounces Parmesan cheese, grated

PER SERVING
Calories: 373; Total carbs: 12g; Net carbs: 9g; Fiber: 3g; Fat: 21g; Protein: 38g; Sodium: 869mg

Sweet, succulent shrimp flavored with lemon, herbs, and garlic have heady aromas and taste bud–pleasing flavors. Scampi is easy to make yet so satisfying. This makeover uses zucchini in place of the spaghetti to sop up all the flavors from the tasty sauce.

1 Using a vegetable peeler, cut the zucchini into long ribbons. Then cut the ribbons into spaghetti-like strips. Set aside.

2 In a large skillet over medium-high heat, heat the olive oil.

3 Add the shallot. Cook for about 5 minutes, stirring occasionally, until soft.

4 Add the shrimp. Cook for about 5 minutes, stirring occasionally, until pink.

5 Add the garlic. Cook for 30 to 60 seconds, stirring constantly, until fragrant.

6 Stir in the zucchini, lemon juice, lemon zest, white wine (if using), salt, pepper, and chicken broth. Simmer for about 5 minutes, or until the zucchini softens and the liquid reduces slightly.

7 Stir in the parsley.

8 Top with the Parmesan cheese, and serve.

TIMESAVING TIP: Zucchini works well in all types of spiral slicers. Instead of cutting the zucchini by hand, use a spiral slicer to save some time.

LINGUINE WITH CLAM SAUCE

SERVES 4 ■ PREP TIME: 10 MINUTES ■ COOK TIME: 15 MINUTES

GF

4 zucchini

4 tablespoons unsalted butter

1 onion, diced

5 garlic cloves

2 (5-ounce) cans clams, undrained

Juice of 1 lemon

⅛ teaspoon red pepper flakes

1 teaspoon dried oregano

½ teaspoon salt

¼ teaspoon freshly ground black pepper

2 tablespoons chopped fresh basil

2 tablespoons chopped fresh Italian parsley

4 ounces Parmesan cheese, grated

PER SERVING
Calories: 279; Total carbs: 21g; Net carbs: 18g; Fiber: 3g; Fat: 18g; Protein: 14g; Sodium: 841mg

Sweet clams and a cheesy sauce are delicious with pasta. When you get a taste for seafood pasta, this recipe comes together quickly for fast satisfaction. Using canned clams with juice makes the prep easy.

1 Using a vegetable peeler, cut the zucchini into ribbon-like strips. Then, cut them into linguine-size ribbons. Alternatively, use a spiral slicer to cut the zucchini into noodles. Set aside.

2 In a large skillet over medium-high heat, heat the butter.

3 Add the onion. Cook for about 5 minutes, stirring occasionally, or until soft.

4 Add the garlic. Cook for 30 to 60 seconds, stirring constantly, until fragrant.

5 Add the clams, lemon juice, red pepper flakes, oregano, salt, pepper, and zucchini. Cook for about 5 minutes, stirring occasionally, until the zucchini softens.

6 Stir in the basil and parsley.

7 Top with the Parmesan cheese, and serve.

FETTUCCINE ALFREDO

SERVES 4 ▪ PREP TIME: 10 MINUTES ▪ COOK TIME: 10 MINUTES

FOR THE PASTA

4 zucchini

2 tablespoons extra-virgin olive oil

¼ teaspoon salt

¼ teaspoon freshly ground black pepper

FOR THE ALFREDO SAUCE

4 tablespoons unsalted butter

8 ounces cream cheese

½ cup heavy (whipping) cream

6 ounces Parmesan cheese, grated

PER SERVING
Calories: 579; Total carbs: 10g; Net carbs: 8g; Fiber: 2g; Fat: 53g; Protein: 21g; Sodium: 817mg

Fettuccine Alfredo is like grown-up macaroni and cheese—no wonder it's a favorite. This satisfyingly cheesy dish comes together quickly and tastes so good, you won't notice the missing carbs.

TO MAKE THE PASTA

1 Using a vegetable peeler, cut the zucchini into ribbon-like strips. Then, cut the strips into fettuccine-size ribbons.

2 In a large skillet over medium-high heat, heat the olive oil until it shimmers.

3 Add the zucchini, salt, and pepper. Cook for about 5 minutes, stirring occasionally, until the zucchini softens.

TO MAKE THE ALFREDO SAUCE

1 In a large saucepan over medium heat, stir together the butter, cream cheese, heavy cream, and Parmesan cheese. Cook for about 5 minutes, stirring constantly, until the sauce is blended and all the cheese has melted.

2 Pour the sauce over the zucchini noodles, and serve.

WHY IT WORKS: Fettuccine Alfredo has a few carb traps. The pasta is the obvious one, but traditional Alfredo sauce also has a significant amount of carbs because it usually starts with a flour and butter roux. This low-carb, full-fat version eliminates the flour while maintaining the creamy consistency of the original.

MACARONI AND CHEESE

SERVES 4 ▪ PREP TIME: 10 MINUTES ▪ COOK TIME: 25 MINUTES

GF **V**

1 head cauliflower, cut into florets

1 recipe Alfredo Sauce (page 117)

1 teaspoon Dijon mustard

½ teaspoon garlic powder

6 ounces sharp Cheddar
cheese, grated

¼ teaspoon freshly ground
black pepper

4 tablespoons butter, melted

½ cup almond flour

½ teaspoon salt

PER SERVING
Calories: 800; Total carbs: 9g;
Net carbs: 7g; Fiber: 2g; Fat: 73g;
Protein: 31g; Sodium: 1,469mg

When you want to eat like a kid again, or feed the kids, it's not unusual to want some creamy macaroni and cheese. Topped with crispy bread crumbs and baked in the oven until hot and bubbly, this dish brings back memories of the flavors of childhood. Reward your grown-up low-carb-eating self with this modified, but still delicious, treat.

1 Preheat the oven to 375°F.

2 Bring a large pot of water to a boil over high heat. Add the cauliflower, and cook for about 5 minutes, or until slightly soft.

3 Drain the cauliflower, and transfer it to a 9-inch square baking dish.

4 In a medium pot over medium heat, stir together the Alfredo Sauce, Dijon mustard, garlic powder, Cheddar cheese, and pepper. Cook for about 5 minutes, stirring constantly, or until the cheese melts and blends into the sauce and the sauce is heated through.

5 Pour the sauce over the cauliflower.

6 In a small bowl, stir together the melted butter, almond flour, and salt.

7 Sprinkle over the casserole.

8 Bake for about 15 minutes, or until hot and bubbly, and serve.

WHY IT WORKS: Cauliflower has a fairly neutral flavor that mimics macaroni. It soaks up the flavors of the cheese. The almond flour adds the crunch. You add the memories.

SPAGHETTI CARBONARA

SERVES 4 ▪ PREP TIME: 10 MINUTES ▪ COOK TIME: 15 MINUTES

`GF`

4 zucchini

6 bacon slices, cut into pieces

1 onion, chopped

3 garlic cloves, minced

¼ cup dry white wine

⅛ teaspoon red pepper flakes

3 large eggs, beaten

½ cup heavy (whipping) cream

½ teaspoon salt

¼ teaspoon freshly ground
  black pepper

4 ounces Parmesan cheese, grated

PER SERVING
Calories: 300; Total carbs: 12g; Net
carbs: 9g; Fiber: 3g; Fat: 19g; Protein:
20g; Sodium: 847mg

Bacon-and-egg lovers rejoice—there's a pasta for that. Spaghetti carbonara is salty and a little bit spicy, with classic breakfast flavors of bacon and eggs. What could be better? A carb-friendly version! Best of all, this recipe comes together quickly, so you can satisfy your craving right away.

1 Using a vegetable peeler, cut the zucchini into ribbons. Then, cut the ribbons into strips. Alternatively, use a spiral slicer to cut the zucchini into spaghetti-like strips. Set aside.

2 In a large skillet over medium-high heat, cook the bacon for about 5 minutes, stirring occasionally, until crisp.

3 Using a slotted spoon, transfer the bacon from the rendered fat to a paper towel–lined plate and set aside.

4 To the bacon fat in the skillet, add the onion. Cook, for about 5 minutes, stirring occasionally, until soft.

5 Add the garlic. Cook for 30 to 60 seconds, stirring constantly, until fragrant.

6 Stir in the wine and red pepper flakes, scraping up any browned bits from the bottom of the pan.

7 Add the zucchini. Cook for about 4 minutes, stirring occasionally, until soft.

8 In a small bowl, whisk together the eggs, heavy cream, salt, and pepper.

9 Return the bacon to the skillet, and remove the skillet from the heat.

10 Stir in the egg mixture, allowing the residual heat of the pan to cook it slightly.

11 Top with the Parmesan cheese, and serve.

SPAGHETTI AND MEATBALLS

SERVES 4 ▪ PREP TIME: 10 MINUTES ▪ COOK TIME: 40 MINUTES

`GF`

FOR THE MEATBALLS

½ pound ground beef

½ pound Italian sausage

½ cup almond flour

1 egg, beaten

2 garlic cloves, minced

1 teaspoon dried oregano

1 teaspoon salt

¼ teaspoon freshly ground
black pepper

Pinch red pepper flakes

FOR THE SPAGHETTI

4 zucchini

2 tablespoons extra-virgin
olive oil

FOR THE RED SAUCE

2 tablespoons extra-virgin
olive oil

1 onion, chopped

3 garlic cloves, minced

¼ cup dry white wine (optional)

1 (15-ounce) can crushed
tomatoes, undrained

1 teaspoon dried oregano

½ teaspoon salt

¼ teaspoon red pepper flakes

¼ cup chopped fresh
Italian parsley

4 ounces Parmesan cheese, grated

PER SERVING
Calories: 652; Total carbs: 22g;
Net carbs: 15g; Fiber: 5g; Fat: 43g;
Protein: 43g; Sodium: 1,843mg

When most people think "pasta," they think spaghetti and meatballs. Big, juicy flavorful meatballs atop a spicy marinara make for a tasty Italian meal regularly served on dinner tables around the world. Now, you can serve this dish at your low-carb dinner table and think, "Delicious."

TO MAKE THE MEATBALLS

1 Preheat the oven to 425°F.

2 Line a rimmed baking sheet with parchment paper.

3 In a large bowl, using your hands, mix the ground beef, Italian sausage, almond flour, egg, garlic, oregano, salt, pepper, and red pepper flakes until well blended. Roll into 1-inch meatballs, and put them on the prepared baking sheet.

4 Bake for 15 to 20 minutes, or until cooked.

TO MAKE THE SPAGHETTI

1 Using a vegetable peeler, cut the zucchini into ribbons. Then, cut the ribbons into pasta-like strips. Alternatively, use a spiral slicer to cut the zucchini into spaghetti-like strips.

2 In a large skillet over medium-high heat, heat the olive oil until it shimmers.

3 Add the zucchini. Cook for about 5 minutes, stirring occasionally, until al dente.

1 In another large skillet over medium-high heat, heat the olive oil until it shimmers.

2 Add the onion. Cook for about 5 minutes, stirring occasionally, until soft.

3 Add the garlic. Cook for 30 to 60 seconds, stirring constantly, until fragrant.

4 Stir in the white wine (if using). Cook, stirring, for 1 minute.

5 Add the tomatoes, oregano, salt, red pepper flakes, and parsley. Cook for about 5 minutes, stirring occasionally, until thick and saucy.

6 Add the zucchini noodles to the sauce, and cook for 1 to 2 minutes to reheat them.

7 Top with the meatballs and Parmesan cheese, and serve.

CANNELLONI

SERVES 4 ▪ PREP TIME: 10 MINUTES ▪ COOK TIME: 1 HOUR

GF V

4 zucchini
8 ounces full-fat ricotta cheese
½ cup pesto
1 recipe Red Sauce (page 120)
6 ounces fresh mozzarella, sliced

PER SERVING
Calories: 498; Total carbs: 26g;
Net carbs: 19g; Fiber: 7g; Fat: 33g;
Protein: 27g; Sodium: 1,038mg

Cannelloni typically features a rich, cheesy filling stuffed inside rolls of pasta. This vegetarian version gets additional flavor from pesto sauce mixed with the ricotta cheese. The dish features two types of cheese, making it savory and rich.

1 Preheat the oven to 350°F.

2 Using a vegetable peeler, slice the zucchini into wide ribbons. Then, cut the ribbons in half crosswise.

3 In a small bowl, mix the ricotta cheese and pesto until well combined.

4 In a 9-inch square baking dish, lay 3 zucchini ribbons side by side, overlapping slightly.

5 Spoon 2 tablespoons of the ricotta-pesto mixture onto the zucchini. Roll the zucchini around the filling. Repeat with the remaining zucchini and ricotta filling until all the filling is used.

6 Pour the Red Sauce over the rolls, and top with the mozzarella cheese slices.

7 Bake for 45 minutes to 1 hour, or until the cheese is brown and bubbly, and serve.

LASAGNA

SERVES 4 ▪ PREP TIME: 15 MINUTES ▪ COOK TIME: 1 HOUR, PLUS 10 MINUTES RESTING TIME

GF

1 pound bulk Italian sausage
8 ounces Swiss cheese, grated
4 ounces Parmesan cheese, grated
4 zucchini
1 recipe Red Sauce (page 120)
8 ounces full-fat ricotta cheese

PER SERVING
Calories: 933; Total carbs: 26g;
Net carbs: 19g; Fiber: 7g; Fat: 65g;
Protein: 58g; Sodium: 1,811mg

Cheesy and bubbly, lasagna tops many people's cravings list. With a spicy red sauce, savory ground meat, and three kinds of cheese, this layered dish is satisfying and delicious. This recipe follows fairly closely to the original, replacing the pasta noodles with zucchini.

1 In a large skillet over medium-high heat, cook the Italian sausage for 5 to 7 minutes, crumbling with a spoon, until browned. Set aside.

2 In a small bowl, mix together the Swiss cheese and Parmesan cheese.

3 Preheat the oven to 350°F.

4 If you have a mandolin, slice one zucchini into thin rounds, and the remaining 3 zucchini into wide ribbons using a vegetable peeler. If you don't have a mandolin, slice all 4 zucchini into ribbons.

5 Spread one-third of the Red Sauce over the bottom of a 9-inch square baking dish.

6 Lay down several zucchini ribbons, overlapping slightly, to cover the sauce.

7 Spread half of the ricotta cheese over the zucchini. Sprinkle half the sausage over the ricotta. Then sprinkle with one-third of the Swiss and Parmesan mixture.

8 Repeat steps 5 through 7 one more time.

9 Top with final layer of zucchini ribbons, the remaining sauce, and the remaining Swiss and Parmesan mixture.

10 Bake for 45 minutes to 1 hour, or until the cheese is brown and bubbly.

11 Remove from the oven, and let rest for 10 minutes before serving.

CASSEROLES AND NOODLES

MOUSSAKA

SERVES 4 ▪ PREP TIME: 15 MINUTES, PLUS 30 MINUTES TO DRAIN ▪ COOK TIME: 1 HOUR

GF

1 eggplant, peeled and cut into ¼-inch-thick slices

1 tablespoon plus 1 teaspoon salt, divided

Cooking spray

2 tablespoons extra-virgin olive oil

½ pound ground lamb

½ onion, chopped

2 garlic cloves, minced

1 (14-ounce) can crushed tomatoes, undrained

¼ teaspoon ground nutmeg

¼ teaspoon ground cinnamon

¼ teaspoon ground cloves

¼ teaspoon dried oregano

¼ teaspoon freshly ground black pepper

1 recipe Alfredo Sauce (page 117)

PER SERVING
Calories: 686; Total carbs: 20g; Net carbs: 12g; Fiber: 8g; Fat: 54g; Protein: 34g; Sodium: 1,376mg

An eggplant and potato dish fragrant with Mediterranean spices and topped with bubbly cheese, moussaka has a taste and texture that leaves people wanting more. This carb-friendly makeover will fill your kitchen with deliciously enticing fragrances as it cooks. Everyone will be on time for dinner tonight!

1 In a colander placed over the sink, sprinkle the eggplant with 1 tablespoon salt. Let sit for about 30 minutes so the salt can draw out the water.

2 Coat a 9-inch square baking dish with cooking spray. Set aside.

3 Preheat the oven to 350°F.

4 Using a paper towel, wipe the eggplant dry, removing any salt and moisture.

5 Brush both sides of the eggplant slices with the olive oil. Place in a single layer on a nonstick baking sheet, and bake for 10 to 15 minutes, or until tender. Remove from the oven, and set aside. Leave the oven on.

6 In a large skillet over medium-high heat, cook the lamb for about 5 minutes, crumbling with a spoon, until browned.

7 Add the onion. Cook for 5 minutes, until soft.

8 Add the garlic. Cook for 30 to 60 seconds, stirring constantly, until fragrant.

9 Stir in the tomatoes, nutmeg, cinnamon, cloves, oregano, the remaining 1 teaspoon of salt, and pepper. Reduce the heat to low. Cook for about 10 minutes, stirring occasionally, or until thickened.

10 Line the bottom of the prepared dish with the roasted eggplant, and top with the lamb mixture.

11 Pour the Alfredo Sauce over the lamb.

12 Bake for about 20 minutes, or until hot and bubbly, and serve.

WHY IT WORKS: There's no need to add carb-filled potatoes to this dish because the eggplant has a similar taste and texture. Salting the eggplant draws out bitter liquids, making it taste even more like potatoes.

SHRIMP CURRY

SERVES 4 ▪ PREP TIME: 10 MINUTES ▪ COOK TIME: 20 MINUTES

GF DF

1 head cauliflower, cut into florets

3 tablespoons coconut oil

1 pound medium shrimp, peeled, deveined, and tails removed

½ onion, chopped

2 tablespoons grated fresh ginger

3 garlic cloves, minced

1 teaspoon salt

½ teaspoon freshly ground black pepper

1 tablespoon curry powder

3 carrots, chopped

1 zucchini, chopped

1 (14-ounce) can coconut milk

Juice of 1 lime

¼ cup chopped fresh cilantro

PER SERVING
Calories: 493; Total carbs: 20g; Net carbs: 13g; Fiber: 7g; Fat: 36g; Protein: 30g; Sodium: 914mg

The fragrant spices in curry combined with creamy coconut milk and sweetly succulent shrimp create a flavor combination that leaves you craving more. This simple curry has all the delicious flavor of a typical curry but uses cauliflower in place of high-carb rice.

1 Over a large bowl, grate the cauliflower on a box grater. Set aside.

2 In a large pot over medium-high heat, heat the coconut oil.

3 Add the shrimp. Cook for about 4 minutes, stirring frequently, until pink. Using tongs, remove the shrimp from the oil and set aside.

4 To the pot, add the onion, ginger, garlic, salt, pepper, and curry powder. Cook for about 5 minutes, stirring frequently, until the onions are soft.

5 Add the carrots and zucchini. Cook for 5 minutes more, stirring occasionally, until the vegetables are soft.

6 Return the shrimp to the pan.

7 Stir in the coconut milk, lime juice, and cauliflower. Bring to a simmer. Simmer for 5 minutes.

8 Remove from the heat, stir in the cilantro, and serve.

PAELLA

SERVES 4 ▪ PREP TIME: 10 MINUTES ▪ COOK TIME: 30 MINUTES

GF

1 head cauliflower, cut into florets

2 tablespoons unsalted butter

Pinch saffron threads

1¼ cups hot unsalted chicken broth, divided

3 bacon slices, cut into pieces

4 ounces boneless, skinless chicken thighs, cut into 1-inch pieces

4 ounces chorizo, sliced

½ onion, chopped

1 carrot, chopped

3 garlic cloves, minced

4 ounces shrimp, peeled, deveined, and tails removed

1 teaspoon smoked paprika

½ teaspoon salt

¼ teaspoon freshly ground black pepper

2 tablespoons chopped fresh Italian parsley

PER SERVING
Calories: 412; Total carbs: 9g; Net carbs: 6g; Fiber: 3g; Fat: 27g; Protein: 32g; Sodium: 1,286mg

With saffron-scented rice, succulent seafood, spicy chorizo, and fragrant herbs, paella has something for everyone. This tasty Spanish rice dish is so aromatic and satisfying that it makes many people's list of top cravings. The cauliflower rice here can make this a low-carb solution if it's on your list of top cravings, too.

1 Over a large bowl, grate the cauliflower on a box grater.

2 In a large skillet over medium-high heat, heat the butter.

3 Add the cauliflower. Cook for about 5 minutes, stirring occasionally, until the cauliflower softens.

4 In a small bowl, mix the saffron threads with ¼ cup of hot chicken broth. Add the saffron broth to the cauliflower. Cook for 2 or 3 more minutes, stirring occasionally, until the water evaporates. Remove from the heat, and set aside.

5 In a large pot over medium-high heat, cook the bacon for about 5 minutes, stirring occasionally, until browned.

6 Add the chicken and chorizo. Cook for about 5 minutes, stirring occasionally, until the meat is cooked.

7 Add the onion and carrot. Cook for about 5 minutes more, stirring occasionally, until the vegetables are soft.

8 Add the garlic. Cook for 30 to 60 seconds, stirring constantly, until fragrant.

9 Stir in the remaining 1 cup of hot chicken broth, the shrimp, paprika, salt, and pepper. Cook for about 4 minutes more, stirring occasionally, until the shrimp is pink.

10 Stir in the cauliflower and parsley, and serve immediately.

CHEESY CHICKEN AND RICE

SERVES 4 ▪ PREP TIME: 10 MINUTES ▪ COOK TIME: 50 MINUTES

GF

1 head cauliflower, cut into florets

Salt

Freshly ground black pepper

4 chicken thighs, skin on

4 ounces frozen pearl onions

4 ounces button mushrooms, quartered

1 recipe Cream of Mushroom Soup (page 79)

6 ounces Cheddar cheese, grated

PER SERVING
Calories: 835; Total carbs: 26g; Net carbs: 19g; Fiber: 8g; Fat: 49g; Protein: 69g; Sodium: 1,771mg

Cheesy chicken and rice is like a warm, comforting hug. If you need a hug, try this version. You get all the goodness of the savory chicken, sweet pearl onions, and meaty mushrooms in a creamy, cheesy sauce, but without the traditional rice or carbs. The ingredients meld together into a satisfying, crave-busting meal.

1 Preheat the oven to 375°F.

2 Over a large bowl, grate the cauliflower on a box grater. Spread the cauliflower rice in the bottom of a 9-inch square baking dish.

3 Season the chicken thighs with salt and pepper, and place them on top of the cauliflower.

4 Sprinkle the onions and mushrooms over the chicken.

5 In a large bowl, mix together the Cream of Mushroom Soup and Cheddar cheese. Pour the mixture over the chicken and cauliflower rice.

6 Bake for 50 minutes, or until the chicken is cooked through, and serve.

WHY IT WORKS: This recipe is normally made with condensed canned cream soups, which are high in carbs because they contain a flour and fat roux. Using Cream of Mushroom Soup (page 79) eliminates the carbs usually found in canned soups. Substituting the cauliflower rice for grain rice eliminates the other major source of carbs in the traditional version of this classic dish.

CHICKEN PAD THAI WITH PEANUT SAUCE

SERVES 4 ■ PREP TIME: 10 MINUTES ■ COOK TIME: 55 MINUTES

DF

1 spaghetti squash, halved lengthwise and seeded

2 tablespoons coconut oil

8 ounces boneless, skinless chicken breast, cubed

6 scallions, sliced on the diagonal

2 carrots, thinly sliced on the diagonal

3 garlic cloves, minced

1 recipe Peanut Sauce (page 165)

¼ cup freshly squeezed lime juice

¼ cup chopped peanuts, divided

¼ cup chopped fresh cilantro, divided

¼ cup bean sprouts, divided

PER SERVING
Calories: 393; Total carbs: 20g;
Net carbs: 14g; Fiber: 4g; Fat: 24g;
Protein: 29g; Sodium: 1,053mg

Pad Thai offers an explosion of flavors and textures. It's slightly sweet, salty, nutty, spicy, and fragrant with fresh herbs. Texturally, it's soft, crunchy, and toothsome all at the same time. Is it any wonder that it's so craveable?

1 Preheat the oven to 450°F.

2 Put the spaghetti squash, cut-side up, in a large baking dish. Bake for about 40 minutes, or until tender. Remove from the oven.

3 Using a fork, shred the squash flesh into spaghetti noodles. Set aside.

4 In a large skillet over medium-high heat, heat the coconut oil.

5 Add the chicken. Cook for about 6 minutes, stirring occasionally, until cooked through.

6 Add the scallions and carrots. Cook for 4 to 5 minutes more, stirring occasionally, until the vegetables are crisp-tender.

7 Add the garlic. Cook for 30 to 60 seconds, stirring constantly, until fragrant.

8 In a small bowl, whisk together the Peanut Sauce and lime juice.

9 Stir the sauce into the skillet. Cook for about 2 minutes, or until just heated through.

10 Evenly divide the noodles among 4 bowls. Spoon equal amounts of sauce into each bowl over the noodles.

11 Top each with about 1 tablespoon of peanuts, 1 tablespoon of cilantro, and 1 tablespoon of bean sprouts, and serve.

CHICKEN POTPIE

SERVES 4 ■ PREP TIME: 10 MINUTES ■ COOK TIME: 50 MINUTES

FOR THE FILLING

2 tablespoons unsalted butter

4 ounces pancetta, diced

8 ounces boneless, skinless
  chicken thighs, cubed

Salt

Freshly ground black pepper

½ onion, chopped

1 carrot, chopped

1 celery stalk, chopped

4 ounces button mushrooms,
  quartered

3 garlic cloves, minced

½ recipe Cream of Mushroom
  Soup (page 79)

½ teaspoon dried tarragon

FOR THE CRUST

1 cup almond flour

1½ tablespoons very cold
  unsalted butter, cut into
  small pieces

1 egg

4 ounces Parmesan cheese, grated

½ teaspoon salt

¼ teaspoon freshly ground
  black pepper

PER SERVING
Calories: 692; Total carbs: 17g;
Net carbs: 12g; Fiber: 4g; Fat: 49g;
Protein: 47g; Sodium: 1,965mg

Digging in to chicken potpie on a fall or winter evening is the ultimate in comfort. With a flaky or crumbly crust and a savory chicken and vegetable filling, chicken potpie satisfies your cravings for something warm and soothing. You'll be doubly comforted with this version, as it won't derail your carb counts.

TO MAKE THE FILLING

1 Preheat the oven to 350°F.

2 In a large skillet over medium-high heat, heat the butter.

3 Add the pancetta. Cook for about 5 minutes, stirring occasionally, until browned.

4 Using a slotted spoon, transfer the pancetta from the fat to a plate. Set aside.

5 Season the chicken liberally with salt and pepper, and add it to the fat in the skillet. Cook it for about 5 minutes, stirring occasionally, until cooked through. Using tongs, remove the chicken from the fat. Add it to the plate with the pancetta and set aside.

6 Add the onion, carrot, celery, and mushrooms to the skillet. Cook for about 6 minutes, stirring occasionally, until the vegetables begin to brown.

7 Add the garlic. Cook for 30 to 60 seconds, stirring constantly, until fragrant.

8 Stir in the Cream of Mushroom Soup and tarragon.

9 Return the chicken and pancetta to the pan, along with any accumulated juices on the plate. Bring to a simmer. Remove from the heat and pour into a 9-inch pie plate.

1 In a food processor, quickly pulse together the almond flour, butter, egg, Parmesan cheese, salt, and pepper 10 times, or until it resembles coarse sand.

2 Press the dough into a ball, and put it between 2 sheets of parchment paper. Pressing on the top sheet, flatten the dough into a round. Then, using a rolling pin, roll it out into a ¼-inch-thick round.

3 Peel the parchment away from the dough. Place the dough over the filling. Using your fingers, crimp the edges around the pie plate.

4 Using a sharp knife, cut 3 (1-inch) slits in the center of the dough.

5 Bake for 15 minutes.

6 Reduce the heat to 325°F.

7 Continue baking for about 15 minutes more, or until the pie is golden brown, and serve.

TRY IT THIS WAY: If you don't have a food processor, put the crust ingredients in a bowl and use a pastry cutter or two knifes to cut together the ingredients until they resemble coarse sand. Using a pastry cutter, put it in the mixture and twist several times. Using two butter knives, hold them with the blades facing each other, and pull them away from one another, working at different angles all around the bowl.

CHICKEN ENCHILADAS

SERVES 4 ▪ PREP TIME: 10 MINUTES ▪ COOK TIME: 40 MINUTES

GF

FOR THE SAUCE

2 tablespoons extra-virgin olive oil

½ onion, minced

3 garlic cloves, minced

1 (15-ounce) can tomato sauce

3 tablespoons chili powder

1 teaspoon ground cumin

1 teaspoon ground coriander

½ teaspoon salt

FOR THE CASSEROLE

2 tablespoons extra-virgin olive oil

8 ounces boneless, skinless chicken thighs, cubed

1 onion, chopped

1 green bell pepper, seeded and chopped

1½ cups grated Cheddar cheese

4 scallions, chopped

PER SERVING
Calories: 474; Total carbs: 17g;
Net carbs: 12g; Fiber: 5g; Fat: 34g;
Protein: 30g; Sodium: 1,223mg

If you miss dining out in Mexican restaurants and enjoying cheesy, spicy enchiladas, then you're in luck. You can still have all the flavors and textures of chicken enchiladas, without all the carbs. Try this baked casserole, which gives you all the flavor of enchiladas, minus the tortillas.

TO MAKE THE SAUCE

1 In a large skillet over medium-high heat, heat the olive oil until it shimmers.

2 Add the onion. Cook for about 5 minutes, stirring occasionally, until soft.

3 Add the garlic. Cook for 30 to 60 seconds, stirring constantly, until fragrant.

4 Stir in the tomato sauce, chili powder, cumin, coriander, and salt. Bring to a simmer. Cook for 5 minutes, stirring occasionally, to allow the flavors to blend.

TO MAKE THE CASSEROLE

1 Preheat the oven to 350°F.

2 In another large skillet over medium-high heat, heat the olive oil until it shimmers.

3 Add the chicken. Cook for about 5 minutes, stirring occasionally, until cooked through.

4 Add the onion and green bell pepper. Cook for about 5 minutes more, stirring occasionally, until the vegetables are soft.

5 Transfer the chicken and vegetable mixture to a 9-inch square baking dish.

6 Top with the sauce, and sprinkle with the Cheddar cheese and scallions.

7 Cover the dish with aluminum foil. Bake for about 20 minutes, or until the cheese melts and the casserole is hot, and serve.

TIMESAVING TIP: You don't need to cook your own chicken for these enchiladas. Purchase a precooked rotisserie chicken, shred the meat, and continue with the recipe.

OVEN-FRIED CHICKEN

SERVES 4 ▪ PREP TIME: 10 MINUTES ▪ COOK TIME: 40 MINUTES

GF

4 ounces pork rinds, crushed
    into a powder

1 teaspoon garlic powder

1 teaspoon onion powder

1 teaspoon dried thyme

½ teaspoon salt

½ teaspoon freshly ground
    black pepper

¼ teaspoon cayenne pepper

4 bone-in, skin-on chicken thighs

½ cup (1 stick) unsalted butter,
    melted, divided

PER SERVING
Calories: 649; Total carbs: 1g;
Net carbs: 1g; Fiber: 0g; Fat: 44g;
Protein: 61g; Sodium: 1,127mg

Fried chicken has been the downfall of many diets. With its savory, flavorful, crunchy skin covering hot, juicy chicken, it just leaves you wanting more. Try this tasty oven-fried version with Mashed Potatoes (page 46) for a true comfort meal, without the guilt.

1 Preheat the oven to 400°F.

2 In a large resealable plastic bag, combine the pork rinds, garlic powder, onion powder, thyme, salt, black pepper, and cayenne pepper. Seal and shake until well combined.

3 Brush the chicken with ¼ cup of melted butter. Place it in the bag, seal, and shake vigorously to coat.

4 In a large ovenproof skillet (such as cast iron) over medium-high heat, heat the remaining ¼ cup of butter until it shimmers.

5 Add the chicken. Cook it for about 5 minutes, without stirring, until browned. Flip and cook for 5 minutes more.

6 Transfer the ovenproof skillet to the preheated oven. Cook for about 30 minutes, or until the chicken is cooked through. Blot the chicken on paper towels before serving.

WHY IT WORKS: The pork rinds make a very crispy coating for the chicken. The trick is to pulverize them so they are powdery, with no big chunks left. You can do this in a food processor, or put them in a resealable plastic bag and crush to a powder with a rolling pin.

CHICKEN PARMESAN

SERVES 4 ▪ PREP TIME: 10 MINUTES ▪ COOK TIME: 30 MINUTES

GF

1 pound boneless chicken breast, cut into four pieces

½ cup almond flour

4 ounces pork rinds, crushed

¾ cup Parmesan cheese, grated, divided

1 teaspoon garlic powder

1 teaspoon onion powder

1 teaspoon dried oregano

½ teaspoon salt

¼ teaspoon freshly ground black pepper

2 large eggs, beaten

3 tablespoons extra-virgin olive oil

1 recipe Red Sauce (page 120)

PER SERVING
Calories: 764; Total carbs: 17g;
Net carbs: 12g; Fiber: 5g; Fat: 45g;
Protein: 75g; Sodium: 1,895mg

This baked chicken dish has crispy-coated chicken patties, garlic-scented tomato sauce, and lots of gooey melted cheese. It's traditionally served with carb-loaded spaghetti, but you can make up a batch of zucchini noodles instead, or just enjoy it on its own.

1 Preheat the oven to 450°F.

2 Put each piece of chicken breast meat between two pieces of parchment paper. Using a mallet or rolling pin, flatten the meat to a ½-inch thickness.

3 In a shallow dish, whisk together the almond flour, pork rinds, ¼ cup of Parmesan cheese, the garlic powder, onion powder, oregano, salt, and pepper.

4 In another shallow dish, whisk the eggs until well combined.

5 In a large skillet over medium-high heat, heat the olive oil.

6 Dip the chicken into the beaten eggs, and then into the almond flour mixture. Put the chicken in the hot olive oil. Cook for about 5 minutes per side, or until browned on both sides.

7 Transfer the chicken to a 9-inch square baking dish, and pour the Red Sauce over the top.

8 Top with the remaining ½ cup of Parmesan cheese.

9 Bake for 15 to 20 minutes, or until the cheese bubbles and the chicken is cooked, and serve.

CHEESY HASH BROWN CASSEROLE

SERVES 4 ▪ PREP TIME: 10 MINUTES ▪ COOK TIME: 50 MINUTES

2 summer squash, peeled and grated

1 tablespoon plus ½ teaspoon salt, divided

½ pound ground beef

½ pound ground pork

½ onion, chopped

1 carrot, chopped

½ green bell pepper, chopped

4 ounces mushrooms, sliced

3 garlic cloves, minced

1 teaspoon chopped fresh thyme

2 tablespoons Dijon mustard

2 tablespoons soy sauce

2 tablespoons Worcestershire sauce

¼ teaspoon freshly ground black pepper

6 ounces Cheddar cheese, grated

2 tablespoons unsalted butter, melted

PER SERVING
Calories: 475; Total carbs: 13g;
Net carbs: 10g; Fiber: 3g; Fat: 26g;
Protein: 46g; Sodium: 1,343mg

Golden-brown hash browns make a perfect crispy topping for a savory ground beef filling. This casserole shuns traditional potato hash browns and offers up beautiful summer squash instead, which also delivers a great buttery-golden crunch, without all the carbs.

1 Preheat the oven to 375°F.

2 In a colander placed over the sink or a bowl, sprinkle the summer squash with 1 tablespoon of salt. Let sit for the salt to draw out water from the squash, while you prepare the filling.

3 In a large skillet over medium-high heat, cook the ground beef and ground pork for about 5 minutes, crumbling with a spoon, until browned.

4 Add the onion, carrot, green bell pepper, and mushrooms. Cook for about 5 minutes, stirring occasionally, until the vegetables are soft.

5 Add the garlic. Cook for 30 to 60 seconds, stirring constantly, until fragrant.

6 In a small bowl, whisk together the thyme, Dijon mustard, soy sauce, Worcestershire sauce, remaining ½ teaspoon of salt, and the pepper. Add to the meat. Cook for 1 minute, stirring to combine.

7 Transfer the meat to a 9-inch square baking dish. Add the Cheddar cheese, and stir to combine.

8 Using paper towels, blot away the excess salt and moisture from the summer squash. Place it in a small bowl. Add the butter, and toss to coat. Cover the meat and cheese mixture with the squash.

9 Bake for about 40 minutes, or until the cheese bubbles and the squash is golden, and serve.

TAMALE PIE

SERVES 4 ■ PREP TIME: 10 MINUTES ■ COOK TIME: 35 MINUTES

GF

FOR THE FILLING

1 pound ground beef

1 onion, chopped

1 green bell pepper

1 (15-ounce) can crushed tomatoes, undrained

1 teaspoon garlic powder

2 tablespoons chili powder

½ teaspoon ground cumin

Dash cayenne pepper

½ teaspoon salt

¼ teaspoon freshly ground black pepper

FOR THE CRUST

½ cup almond meal

4 ounces pork rinds, crushed into a powder

1 egg

¼ cup water

¼ teaspoon stevia

½ teaspoon chili powder

¼ teaspoon salt

6 ounces Cheddar cheese, grated

PER SERVING

Calories: 708; Total carbs: 19g; Net carbs: 11g; Fiber: 8g; Fat: 39g; Protein: 71g; Sodium: 1,588mg

Traditional tamale pie has a golden-brown carb-laden corn crust on top. It blends perfectly with the tomato and ground beef layer underneath, which is fragrant with onions, garlic, cumin, and other southwestern spices. Make this version instead, and celebrate the southwestern flavors you crave, without the diet-busting carbs.

TO MAKE THE FILLING

1 Preheat the oven to 350°F.

2 In a large skillet over medium-high heat, cook the ground beef for about 5 minutes, crumbling with a spoon, until browned.

3 Add the onion and green bell pepper. Cook for about 5 minutes more, stirring occasionally, until the vegetables are soft.

4 Stir in the crushed tomatoes, garlic powder, chili powder, cumin, cayenne pepper, salt, and black pepper. Bring to a simmer. Cook for about 5 minutes more, stirring occasionally, until the liquid reduces.

5 Transfer the mixture to a 9-inch square baking dish.

TO MAKE THE CRUST

1 In a large bowl, mix together the almond meal, pork rinds, egg, water, stevia, chili powder, salt, and Cheddar cheese until well combined.

2 Spread over the meat mixture, pressing down to hold it together.

3 Bake for about 20 minutes, or until the crust turns golden.

WHY IT WORKS: Since the almond flour and pork rinds aren't as sweet as fresh corn, adding a bit of stevia gives the crust the same sweetness you find in a cornmeal crust—but without the carbs.

TATER TOT CASSEROLE

SERVES 4 ▪ PREP TIME: 10 MINUTES ▪ COOK TIME: 1 HOUR

1 teaspoon salt, divided, plus additional for seasoning

1 head cauliflower, broken into small florets

1 pound ground beef

1 onion, chopped

6 ounces button mushrooms, quartered

3 garlic cloves, minced

1 recipe Cream of Mushroom Soup (page 79)

2 tablespoons Worcestershire sauce

1 teaspoon garlic powder

1 teaspoon dried thyme

¼ teaspoon freshly ground black pepper

2 tablespoons butter, melted

PER SERVING
Calories: 656; Total carbs: 28g; Net carbs: 20g; Fiber: 8g; Fat: 37g; Protein: 50g; Sodium: 1,658mg

Remember as a kid when tater tot casserole was a huge treat? The crispy tater tots were little pillows of starchy goodness floating atop a creamy casserole of ground beef and mushrooms. This recipe will take you back to child-hood, allowing you to relive one of your favorite childhood meals as a carb-counting adult.

1 Preheat the oven to 400°F.

2 To a large pot of boiling water, add a dash of salt.

3 Add the cauliflower. Cook for 5 minutes. Drain and trans-fer to paper towels. Set aside to dry.

4 In a large skillet over medium-high heat, cook the ground beef for about 5 minutes, crumbling with a spoon, until browned.

5 Add the onion and mushrooms. Cook for about 5 min-utes, stirring occasionally, until the vegetables are soft.

6 Add the garlic. Cook for 30 to 60 seconds, stirring con-stantly, until fragrant.

7 Stir in the Cream of Mushroom Soup, Worcestershire sauce, garlic powder, thyme, ½ teaspoon of salt, and the pepper.

8 Pour the mixture into a 9-inch square baking dish.

9 Blot any remaining moisture from the cauliflower with paper towels. Add the cauliflower to a large bowl and toss with the melted butter and remaining ½ teaspoon of salt.

10 Spread the cauliflower in an even layer over the ground beef mixture.

11 Bake for 30 to 40 minutes, or until the cauliflower is golden and the filling is hot and bubbly, and serve.

WHY IT WORKS: As always, cauliflower makes a great stand-in, texturally, for potatoes. In this case, making sure the parboiled cauliflower is completely dry and tossing it with butter allows it to turn golden brown in the heat of the oven.

COTTAGE PIE

SERVES 4 ■ PREP TIME: 10 MINUTES ■ COOK TIME: 40 MINUTES

GF

- 1 pound ground lamb
- 1 onion, chopped
- 2 carrots, chopped
- 3 celery stalks, chopped
- 1 zucchini, chopped
- 2 garlic cloves, minced
- 1 cup unsalted chicken broth
- 1 teaspoon dried thyme
- 1 teaspoon garlic powder
- 1 teaspoon salt
- ¼ teaspoon freshly ground black pepper
- 1 recipe Mashed Potatoes (page 45)

PER SERVING
Calories: 400; Total carbs: 13g;
Net carbs: 9g; Fiber: 4g; Fat: 23g;
Protein: 36g; Sodium: 1,132mg

Cottage pie, also known as shepherd's pie, features a delicious mix of minced lamb and savory vegetables, topped with fluffy mashed potatoes. This recipe gives you all the flavor of a delicious traditional cottage pie with far fewer carbs.

1 Preheat the oven to 400°F.

2 In a large skillet over medium-high heat, cook the lamb for about 5 minutes, crumbling with a spoon, until browned.

3 Add the onion, carrots, celery, and zucchini. Cook for about 5 minutes, stirring occasionally, until the vegetables are soft.

4 Add the garlic. Cook for 30 to 60 seconds, stirring constantly, until fragrant.

5 Stir in the chicken broth, thyme, garlic powder, salt, and pepper. Simmer for 5 minutes.

6 Pour the mixture into a 9-inch square baking dish.

7 Spread the Mashed Potatoes on top.

8 Bake for about 25 minutes, or until the top begins to brown, and serve.

WHY IT WORKS: Cottage pie typically contains peas, which are relatively high in carbohydrates. They are omitted here and replaced with zucchini. Likewise, the cauliflower Mashed Potatoes have the texture of potatoes without the starch.

BANGERS AND MASH WITH BEER GRAVY

SERVES 4 ▪ PREP TIME: 10 MINUTES ▪ COOK TIME: 1 HOUR

4 (4-ounce) bratwursts

2 tablespoons unsalted butter

1 onion, thinly sliced

3 garlic cloves, minced

1 teaspoon dried thyme

1 teaspoon salt

1 (12-ounce) bottle low-carb amber beer, such as Michelob Ultra Amber (with fewer than 5g carbs)

5 carrots, chopped

1 cup unsalted chicken broth, plus additional for thinning

1 recipe Mashed Potatoes (page 45)

PER SERVING
Calories: 494; Total carbs: 26g; Net carbs: 20g; Fiber: 5g; Fat: 31g; Protein: 26g; Sodium: 2,320mg

This British pub favorite offers juicy sausages on top of creamy mashed potatoes. It's all covered in a savory onion and beer gravy that gives it mouthwatering flavor. Trimming the carbs takes a little creativity, but this should fulfill your craving for a favorite pub food.

1 Preheat the oven to 350°F.

2 Place a baking rack on a rimmed baking sheet.

3 Put the bratwursts on the rack. Carefully transfer the sheet to the preheated oven, and bake for 1 hour.

4 While the bratwursts cook, in a large skillet over medium-low heat, heat the butter.

5 Add the onion, garlic, thyme, and salt. Cook for about 30 minutes, stirring occasionally, until the onions are caramelized.

6 While the onions cook, in a medium pot over medium-high heat, bring the beer to a boil.

7 Add the carrots. Boil them for about 15 minutes, or until soft. Transfer the carrots and beer to a food processor.

8 Add the chicken broth. Process for about 1 minute, or until puréed.

9 Add the puréed carrots to the caramelized onions to make the gravy. Adjust the thickness with additional chicken broth, if needed.

10 Spoon an equal amount of Mashed Potatoes onto each of 4 plates.

11 Top each with 1 sausage and one-quarter of the gravy, and serve.

WHY IT WORKS: Starchy carrots serve as a thickener for the gravy, eliminating the need for high-carb flour.

CHAPTER 9

DESSERTS

VANILLA MILK SHAKE

SERVES 4 ▪ PREP TIME: 5 MINUTES

GF V

1 cup crushed ice
½ cup heavy (whipping) cream
½ cup unsweetened almond milk
1 teaspoon vanilla extract
1 teaspoon stevia

PER SERVING
Calories: 495; Total carbs: 9g;
Net carbs: 6g; Fiber: 3g; Fat: 51g;
Protein: 4g; Sodium: 41mg

Creamy, sweet, cold, and refreshing, vanilla milk shakes are a simple yet delicious treat. The best part is that you can customize yours with different flavors—add cocoa powder for chocolate, or other flavored extracts such as almond or mint—to make a tasty low-carb dessert.

In a blender, blend the ice, heavy cream, almond milk, vanilla, and stevia on high for 2 minutes, and serve.

TRY IT THIS WAY: Make a chocolate-mint shake by adding ¼ teaspoon mint extract and 2 tablespoons coconut powder.

CHOCOLATE PUDDING

SERVES 2 ▪ PREP TIME: 5 MINUTES

GF V

2 avocados, pitted and peeled

¼ cup coconut milk

¼ cup cocoa powder

2 tablespoons Maple Syrup
(page 164)

1 teaspoon stevia

1 teaspoon vanilla extract

Pinch salt

PER SERVING
Calories: 509; Total carbs: 25g;
Net carbs: 8g; Fiber: 17g; Fat: 48g;
Protein: 6g; Sodium: 19mg

When only pudding will soothe that sweet tooth, this smooth and creamy, rich and chocolaty dish will not disappoint. Best of all, you can have it in less than 5 minutes. When that chocolate craving hits—and you know it will—this is a great low-carb way to satisfy it.

In a food processor, blend the avocado, coconut milk, cocoa powder, Maple Syrup, stevia, vanilla, and salt until smooth, and serve.

WHY IT WORKS: Avocado makes a perfect pudding base because it is so creamy and fatty. While avocados are high in carbs, they are also high in fiber, so the net carbs end up being quite low.

SNICKERDOODLES

MAKES 24 ■ PREP TIME: 10 MINUTES, PLUS 10 MINUTES TO CHILL ■ COOK TIME: 10 MINUTES

`GF` `V`

2½ cups almond flour

1 teaspoon cream of tartar

1 teaspoon baking soda

Pinch salt

½ cup (1 stick) unsalted butter, at room temperature

1½ cups sweetener (Truvia Baking Blend or Swerve), divided

2 large eggs, beaten

1 teaspoon vanilla extract

2 tablespoons ground cinnamon

PER SERVING (1 cookie)
Calories: 88; Total carbs: 13g; Net carbs: 12g; Fiber: 1g; Fat: 6g; Protein: 1g; Sodium: 93mg

There are a lot of great things about snickerdoodles. They have a tender, crumbly texture. They are also sweet and slightly tart. Best of all, they are topped with tasty cinnamon sugar that makes them fragrant and delicious. Fill your cookie jar with this lower-carb version, and watch them disappear.

1 Preheat the oven to 350°F.

2 Line a baking sheet with parchment paper.

3 In a medium bowl, sift together the almond flour, cream of tartar, baking soda, and salt. Set aside.

4 In a large bowl, cream together the butter and 1¼ cups of sweetener for 1 to 2 minutes, or until well blended.

5 Add the eggs and vanilla. Continue mixing for 1 to 2 minutes more, until fluffy.

6 Stir in the flour mixture, stirring until combined.

7 Refrigerate the dough for 10 minutes.

8 In a small bowl, mix together the remaining ¼ cup of sweetener and the cinnamon.

9 Roll the dough into 24 balls, and roll each ball in the cinnamon sugar.

10 Put the cookies on a baking sheet about 1 inch apart.

11 Bake for about 10 minutes, or until browned, and serve.

TIMESAVING TIP: These cookies freeze well, and so does the dough. You can either bake an entire batch of cookies and freeze them in a resealable freezer-safe bag, or freeze the dough balls and bake them as you need them.

PEANUT BUTTER COOKIES

MAKES 16 ■ PREP TIME: 10 MINUTES ■ COOK TIME: 15 MINUTES

1 cup peanut butter

1 cup sweetener (Truvia Baking Blend or Swerve)

1 egg, beaten

1 teaspoon vanilla extract

Pinch salt

PER SERVING (1 cookie)
Calories: 129; Total carbs: 15g; Net carbs: 14g; Fiber: 1g; Fat: 8g; Protein: 4g; Sodium: 90mg

Crispy on the outside and chewy on the inside, these peanut butter cookies are so easy to make, and they are full of sweet peanut butter flavor. With just five ingredients, you can have a crave-busting batch of cookies ready to go in less than 30 minutes.

1 Preheat the oven to 350°F.

2 Line a baking sheet with parchment paper.

3 In a medium bowl, mix together the peanut butter, sweetener, egg, vanilla, and salt until well blended.

4 Drop the batter by the tablespoonful onto the prepared baking sheet.

5 Bake for 10 to 12 minutes, or until browned, and serve.

PEANUT BUTTER CUPS

MAKES 12 ▪ PREP TIME: 10 MINUTES ▪ COOK TIME: 5 MINUTES

8 ounces unsweetened baking chocolate

½ cup peanut butter

¼ cup coconut oil

1 teaspoon stevia

Pinch salt

PER SERVING (1 candy)
Calories: 223; Total carbs: 8g;
Net carbs: 3g; Fiber: 5g; Fat: 19g;
Protein: 5g; Sodium: 61mg

Do you love peanut butter cups? This deeply chocolate candy with a hint of peanut butter will satisfy your craving when nothing else will do. It also freezes well, so freeze bite-size pieces in a resealable freezer-safe bag so you can have them handy when a craving hits.

1 Set out 12 mini cupcake liners.

2 In a medium saucepan over medium-low heat, melt together the chocolate, peanut butter, coconut oil, stevia, and salt, stirring constantly, for about 5 minutes.

3 Spoon equal amounts into the liners.

4 Cool at room temperature until hard, and serve. Refrigerate or freeze leftovers for later.

TIMESAVING TIP: If you crave this often, make a double or triple batch. Keep them in the freezer so you have one ready whenever you need a quick fix.

PEPPERMINT PATTIES

MAKES 18 ▪ PREP TIME: 15 MINUTES, PLUS 1 HOUR TO FREEZE ▪
COOK TIME: 5 MINUTES, PLUS 2 HOURS CHILLING TIME

½ cup plus 3 tablespoons
   coconut oil

1 teaspoon peppermint extract

2 teaspoons stevia, divided

2 teaspoons heavy
   (whipping) cream

10 ounces unsweetened
   baking chocolate

PER SERVING (1 candy)
Calories: 153; Total carbs: 5g;
Net carbs: 5g; Fiber: 0g; Fat: 17g;
Protein: 2g; Sodium: 4mg

When the need for that sweet chocolate and cooling mint sensation arises, these candies hit the spot. These candy treats will tingle your taste buds without breaking your carb budget. They're quick and easy to prepare, but plan ahead to allow for chilling and freezing time.

1 Line a large platter with parchment paper.

2 In a small bowl, mix together the ½ cup coconut oil, the peppermint extract, 1 teaspoon of stevia, and the heavy cream.

3 Scoop the mixture by the scant tablespoonful onto the parchment, and flatten with the back of the spoon.

4 Freeze the platter for 1 hour.

5 In a small saucepan over medium-low heat, combine the baking chocolate, the remaining 1 teaspoon of stevia, and the remaining 3 tablespoons of coconut oil. Cook for about 2 minutes, stirring constantly, until melted and well combined. Allow to cool slightly.

6 Dip the frozen peppermint bits into the chocolate, coating completely. Place on a parchment-lined platter.

7 Refrigerate for 1 to 2 hours, or freeze for 30 minutes, until hard, and serve.

WHY IT WORKS: Freezing the filling keeps it solid when you dip it into the warm chocolate, which keeps the coconut oil from melting into a mushy mess.

COFFEE ICE CREAM

SERVES 2 ▪ PREP TIME: 15 MINUTES, PLUS 3 HOURS TO FREEZE

GF V

1 cup **heavy (whipping) cream**
½ cup **strongly brewed coffee**, cooled
1 teaspoon **vanilla extract**
1 teaspoon **stevia**
Pinch **salt**

PER SERVING
Calories: 213; Total carbs: 2g;
Net carbs: 2g; Fiber: 0g; Fat: 22g;
Protein: 1g; Sodium: 102mg

Whether you want to eat it by itself or add it to a coffee drink for a summer chiller, coffee ice cream is sweet, creamy, and fragrant with the aroma of coffee. Use a high-quality coffee for the best flavor.

1 Line a 9-inch square glass pan with parchment paper.

2 In a medium bowl, whisk together the heavy cream, coffee, vanilla, stevia, and salt.

3 Pour the ice cream base into the prepared pan.

4 Freeze for at least 3 hours, or until solid.

5 Remove from the freezer and let the ice cream sit at room temperature for 20 minutes.

6 Peel the parchment away from the ice cream. Break the ice cream into pieces, and put them in a food processor. Process for 20 to 30 seconds, or until smooth.

7 Serve immediately.

TIMESAVING TIP: You can make this ahead of time and keep it in the freezer; just don't process it until right before you serve it. If freezing it for more than a few hours, cover the baking dish with plastic wrap.

STRAWBERRY ICE CREAM

SERVES 4 ※ PREP TIME: 15 MINUTES, PLUS 1 HOUR TO CHILL ※
COOK TIME: 5 MINUTES, PLUS 6 HOURS FREEZING TIME

GF

2 tablespoons cold water

1 teaspoon gelatin

¼ cup coconut milk

¾ cup heavy (whipping) cream, divided

1 teaspoon stevia

½ teaspoon vanilla extract

Pinch salt

1 cup sliced fresh strawberries

PER SERVING
Calories: 131; Total carbs: 4g;
Net carbs: 3g; Fiber: 1g; Fat: 12g;
Protein: 3g; Sodium: 54mg

Early summer, when strawberries are at their peak of ripeness, is the perfect time to make strawberry ice cream. Creamy and sweet, homemade strawberry ice cream is one of summer's greatest pleasures.

1 In a small cup, mix together the water and gelatin. Set aside to bloom.

2 In a medium saucepan over low heat, stir together the coconut milk, 2 tablespoons of heavy cream, the stevia, and vanilla. Stir constantly for about 3 minutes, or until it simmers. Remove from the heat.

3 Stir in the gelatin and salt.

4 Pour the mixture into a bowl. Refrigerate for 1 hour, whisking once or twice during that time.

5 Remove from the refrigerator, and stir in the strawberries.

6 In a large bowl, whip the remaining 10 tablespoons of heavy cream until peaks begin to form.

7 Carefully fold the chilled ice cream mixture into the whipped cream.

8 Freeze for at least 6 hours, removing the ice cream from the freezer and whisking at least twice during that time, and serve.

LEMON SQUARES

MAKES 9 ▪ PREP TIME: 15 MINUTES ▪ COOK TIME: 35 MINUTES, PLUS 30 MINUTES COOLING TIME

GF V

½ cup sweetener (Truvia Baking Blend or Swerve), divided

¾ cup plus 2 tablespoons almond flour, divided

1 tablespoon coconut flour

¼ teaspoon salt

4 tablespoons very cold unsalted butter, roughly chopped

½ cup freshly squeezed lemon juice

2 tablespoons water

1½ teaspoons lemon zest

3 large eggs, beaten

¼ cup heavy (whipping) cream

PER SERVING (1 square)
Calories: 161; Total carbs: 14g;
Net carbs: 13g; Fiber: 1g; Fat: 12g;
Protein: 4g; Sodium: 132mg

If you love the sunny taste of lemon, then you probably love lemon squares. They are the perfect combination of sweet and tart with a crunchy crust and bright lemon flavor. This low-carb version is sure to please your palate.

1 Preheat the oven to 350°F.

2 In a food processor, process ¼ cup of sweetener for 1 minute.

3 Add ¾ cup of almond flour, the coconut flour, salt, and butter. Pulse quickly about 10 times, or until a coarse sand-like mixture forms.

4 Press the mixture into the bottom of a 9-inch square baking dish.

5 Bake for 10 to 15 minutes, or until the crust is golden. Remove from the oven, and set aside to cool for 30 minutes. Maintain the oven temperature.

6 In a large bowl, using a hand-held mixer, mix together the lemon juice, water, lemon zest, remaining ¼ cup of sweetener, eggs, heavy cream, and remaining 2 tablespoons of almond flour until well blended.

7 Pour the mixture over the cooled crust.

8 Bake for about 20 minutes, or until the filling sets.

9 Let cool, then cut into 9 squares, and serve.

APPLE CRISP

SERVES 8 ▪ PREP TIME: 15 MINUTES ▪ COOK TIME: 1 HOUR

GF V

FOR THE CRISP

3 sweet-tart apples, such as Granny Smith, peeled, cored, and sliced

½ cup sweetener (Truvia Baking Blend or Swerve), divided

1 teaspoon ground cinnamon

¼ teaspoon ground nutmeg

2 tablespoons freshly squeezed lemon juice

1 teaspoon lemon zest

½ cup almond flour

2 tablespoons coconut flour

½ cup (1 stick) very cold unsalted butter, cut into pieces

¼ teaspoon salt

¼ cup chopped pecans

FOR THE WHIPPED CREAM

¼ cup heavy (whipping) cream

½ teaspoon vanilla extract

½ teaspoon stevia

Pinch salt

PER SERVING
Calories: 266; Total carbs: 23g; Net carbs: 19g; Fiber: 4g; Fat: 22g; Protein: 2g; Sodium: 160mg

Apples reach the peak of ripeness in the fall, which is the best time to make this dessert. With tender sweet-tart apples and a sweet, spicy, crispy crust, this apple dish offers a little taste of heaven, particularly when topped with clouds of vanilla-scented whipped cream.

TO MAKE THE CRISP

1 Preheat the oven to 350°F.

2 In a large bowl, stir together the apples, ¼ cup of sweetener, the cinnamon, nutmeg, lemon juice, and lemon zest.

3 Transfer the mixture to a 9-inch square baking dish.

4 In a food processor, add the remaining sweetener, almond flour, coconut flour, butter, salt, and pecans, and quickly pulse together 10 times.

5 Pour the mixture over the apples.

6 Bake for about 1 hour, or until the apples are soft and the crust is golden.

TO MAKE THE WHIPPED CREAM

1 In a large bowl, using a hand-held mixer, whip the heavy cream until it forms soft peaks.

2 Add the vanilla, stevia, and salt, and whip for about 20 seconds more to combine.

3 Spoon the whipped cream over the apple crisp, cut into 8 slices, and serve.

WHY IT WORKS: Apples are fairly high in carbs, so the secret here is small portions and adjustments, such as sweetener and nuts in place of the traditional sugar and oats.

APPLE FRITTERS

SERVES 8 ▪ PREP TIME: 15 MINUTES ▪ COOK TIME: 5 MINUTES

GF V

Coconut oil, for frying

¼ cup plus 1 tablespoon
    coconut flour

1 teaspoon ground cinnamon

½ teaspoon baking powder

¼ teaspoon ground nutmeg

Pinch salt

3 large eggs

½ cup heavy (whipping) cream

1 teaspoon apple cider vinegar

1 teaspoon stevia

½ apple, peeled, cored,
    and diced

¼ cup sweetener (Truvia Baking
    Blend or Swerve)

PER SERVING (1 fritter)
Calories: 266; Total carbs: 23g;
Net carbs: 19g; Fiber: 4g; Fat: 22g;
Protein: 2g; Sodium: 160mg

Craving a doughnut? Perhaps this deep-fried apple fritter will fill the bill. With a dusting of sugar on the outside and sweet apple flavor on the inside, these fritters will make you glad you picked them instead of the carb-filled doughnut.

1 Fill a large deep pot with about 2 inches of coconut oil. Place it over medium-high heat, and heat the oil until it reaches 375°F on a candy thermometer.

2 In a large bowl, sift together the coconut flour, cinnamon, baking powder, nutmeg, and salt.

3 In another large bowl, whisk together the eggs, heavy cream, apple cider vinegar, and stevia.

4 Add the wet ingredients to the dry ingredients, stirring until just combined.

5 Fold in the apple.

6 Spoon the batter in 8 equal amounts into the hot oil. Fry for about 4 minutes, or until golden on all sides.

7 Using a slotted spoon or skimmer, transfer the fritters to paper towels. Sprinkle with the sweetener, and serve.

PUMPKIN PIE

SERVES 9 ▪ PREP TIME: 15 MINUTES ▪ COOK TIME: 55 MINUTES

GF V

FOR THE CRUST

2¼ cups almond flour

2 tablespoons coconut flour

¼ teaspoon stevia

¼ teaspoon salt

4 tablespoons very cold unsalted
butter, cut into pieces

FOR THE FILLING

2 cups pumpkin purée

1 cup heavy (whipping) cream

2 large eggs

½ cup sweetener (Truvia Baking
Blend or Swerve)

1 teaspoon vanilla extract

1 teaspoon ground cinnamon

¼ teaspoon ground cloves

¼ teaspoon ground allspice

¼ teaspoon salt

PER SERVING (1 square)
Calories: 201; Total carbs: 18g;
Net carbs: 15g; Fiber: 3g; Fat: 15g;
Protein: 4g; Sodium: 196mg

When the holidays roll around, nothing will do for dessert but pumpkin pie. Sweetly scented with spices, pumpkin pie features a flaky crust and creamy pumpkin custard that brings back fond holiday memories. Whether it's Thanksgiving or any other time of year, if you're craving that forbidden pie, these pumpkin pie bars will hit the spot.

TO MAKE THE CRUST

1 Preheat the oven to 350°F.

2 In a food processor fitted with a chopping blade, quickly pulse together the almond flour, coconut flour, stevia, salt, and butter 10 times, or until the mixture resembles coarse sand.

3 Press the mixture into the bottom of a 9-inch square baking dish.

4 Bake for about 10 minutes, or until golden.

5 Remove from the oven, leaving the oven on.

TO MAKE THE FILLING

1 In a large bowl, using a hand-held mixer, beat together the pumpkin, heavy cream, eggs, sweetener, vanilla, cinnamon, cloves, allspice, and salt until well combined.

2 Pour the mixture over the crust, and bake for about 45 minutes, or until the center sets.

3 Remove from the oven and cool.

4 Cut into 9 squares, and serve.

WHY IT WORKS: Portion control and alternative flours drop the carb counts into workable ranges in this recipe. An entire slice of pumpkin pie, even with artificial sweeteners, is going to blow your carb budget. This recipe won't.

VANILLA CUPCAKES WITH CREAM CHEESE FROSTING

MAKES 24 MINI CUPCAKES ▪ PREP TIME: 15 MINUTES ▪ COOK TIME: 15 MINUTES

GF V

FOR THE FROSTING

½ cup cream cheese, at room temperature

1½ cups powdered sweetener (Truvia Baking Blend or Swerve)

7 tablespoons heavy (whipping) cream

1 teaspoon vanilla extract

FOR THE CUPCAKES

1 cup coconut flour

¾ cup sweetener (Truvia Baking Blend or Swerve)

1 tablespoon baking powder

¼ teaspoon salt

7 large eggs, beaten

1 cup coconut milk

½ cup (1 stick) unsalted butter, melted and cooled slightly

1 teaspoon vanilla extract

PER SERVING (1 cupcake)
Calories: 172; Total carbs: 20g;
Net carbs: 18g; Fiber: 2g; Fat: 12g;
Protein: 3g; Sodium: 97mg

If your craving is for moist cake, these vanilla cupcakes will certainly satisfy. The crumbly cupcake and creamy vanilla frosting provide a sweet treat in a portion-controlled mini-cupcake size.

TO MAKE THE FROSTING

1 In a large bowl, cream together the cream cheese and sweetener until blended.

2 Stir in the heavy cream and vanilla.

TO MAKE THE CUPCAKES

1 Preheat the oven to 350°F.

2 Line 24 mini muffin cups with paper cupcake liners.

3 In a large bowl, sift together the coconut flour, sweetener, baking powder, and salt.

4 In another large bowl, whisk together the eggs, coconut milk, butter, and vanilla.

5 Add the wet ingredients to the dry ingredients, folding them together until just combined.

6 Evenly divide the batter among the muffin cups. Bake for about 15 minutes, or until a toothpick inserted in the center comes out clean.

7 Remove the muffins from the oven and cool completely on a wire rack.

8 Spread the frosting over the cooled cupcakes, and serve.

WHY IT WORKS: Powdered sweetener, such as powdered Swerve, is the only product that creates the consistency frosting normally gets from powdered sugar.

NEW YORK CHEESECAKE

SERVES 9 ▪ PREP TIME: 15 MINUTES ▪ COOK TIME: 1 HOUR

`GF` `V`

½ cup almond flour

½ cup plus 3 tablespoons sweetener (Truvia Baking Blend or Swerve), divided

2 tablespoons unsalted butter, melted

20 ounces cream cheese, at room temperature

½ cup sour cream

2 large eggs

2 teaspoons vanilla extract

PER SERVING (1 square) Calories: 332; Total carbs: 17g; Net carbs: 17g; Fiber: 0g; Fat: 12g; Protein: 7g; Sodium: 226mg

New York cheesecake is tangy, sweet, and slightly dense. The creamy texture contrasts with the crispy crust. This version, cheesecake bars, cuts out the sugar and replaces the carb-laden crust with a nut-based one for a delicious low-carb treat.

1 Preheat the oven to 325°F.

2 In a small bowl, mix together the almond flour, the 3 tablespoons of sweetener, and the butter.

3 Press the mixture into the bottom of a 9-inch square dish.

4 In a large bowl, using a hand-held mixer, beat together the cream cheese, remaining ½ cup of sweetener, sour cream, eggs, and vanilla until blended.

5 Pour the mixture over the crust. Bake for 50 minutes to 1 hour, or until the center sets.

6 Remove from the oven and cool completely.

7 Cut the cheesecake into 9 squares, and serve.

FLOURLESS CHOCOLATE CAKE WITH ORANGE WHIPPED CREAM

SERVES 12 ▪ PREP TIME: 15 MINUTES ▪ COOK TIME: 45 MINUTES

GF V

FOR THE WHIPPED CREAM
¼ cup heavy (whipping) cream
½ teaspoon vanilla extract
1 teaspoon stevia
Zest of 1 orange

FOR THE CAKE
Cooking spray
Almond flour, for dusting
4 ounces unsweetened baking chocolate, chopped into small pieces
½ cup (1 stick) unsalted butter
2 tablespoons heavy (whipping) cream
¾ cup sweetener (Truvia Baking Blend or Swerve), divided
2 tablespoons unsweetened cocoa powder
2 teaspoons vanilla extract
6 large eggs, at room temperature

PER SERVING
Calories: 191; Total carbs: 16g;
Net carbs: 14g; Fiber: 2g; Fat: 16g;
Protein: 4g; Sodium: 89mg

If you're craving chocolate, then this light cake is the perfect replacement. Its deep richness is so satisfying, and the lightly scented orange whipped cream helps cut the richness of the chocolate. For this cake, a very little goes a long way to satisfy your craving.

TO MAKE THE WHIPPED CREAM

1 In a large chilled bowl, using a hand-held mixer, beat the heavy cream until it forms soft mounds.

2 Add the vanilla, stevia, and orange zest, and beat for 30 seconds more to combine.

TO MAKE THE CAKE

1 Preheat the oven to 325°F.

2 Coat an 8-inch springform pan with cooking spray. Dust it with almond flour, tapping out any excess.

3 Fill a medium saucepan with 1 inch of water. Place it over medium-high heat, and create a double boiler by placing a glass bowl over the pan, with its bottom slightly above the surface of the water.

4 Add the chocolate, butter, and heavy cream. Cook for about 5 minutes, stirring constantly, until melted. Cool for 5 minutes.

5 In a large bowl, stir together the cooled chocolate, ¼ cup of sweetener, the cocoa powder, and vanilla until well combined.

6 In another large bowl, using a hand-held mixer, beat the eggs for about 6 minutes, or until they form thick ribbons. Continue beating, and gradually add the remaining ½ cup of sweetener. Beat until fully combined.

7 In 3 additions, carefully fold the egg mixture into the chocolate mixture.

8 Pour the batter into the prepared pan. Bake for about 40 minutes, or until nearly set.

9 Remove from the oven and cool completely on a wire rack before releasing the cake from the pan.

10 Cut the cake into 12 wedges, and serve topped with the whipped cream.

CONDIMENTS AND DRESSINGS

MAPLE SYRUP

MAKES 2 CUPS ▪ PREP TIME: 5 MINUTES ▪ COOK TIME: 5 MINUTES

GF V

2 cups water

1½ cups sweetener (Truvia Baking Blend or Swerve)

2 teaspoons maple extract

2 tablespoons unsalted butter

PER SERVING (1 tablespoon)
Calories: 30; Total carbs: 9g;
Net carbs: 9g; Fiber: 0g; Fat: 1g;
Protein: 0g; Sodium: 6mg

Part of what we enjoy so much about pancakes, waffles, and other breakfast foods is the maple syrup. The sweet syrup blends with the starchy goodness in a perfect marriage of flavor, making breakfast many people's favorite meal of the day. You don't have to miss out on the perfect start to your day with this carb-friendly version.

1 In a small saucepan over high heat, combine the water and sweetener. Bring to a boil. Reduce the heat to low, and simmer for 5 minutes, stirring frequently.

2 Stir in the maple extract and butter, stirring until the butter melts.

WHY IT WORKS: The erythritol in the sweetener acts like sugar, forming a simple syrup with water. Swerve is a bit more effective at this than Truvia Baking Blend, but both perform passably. Portion control is essential here. This syrup is best used sparingly.

PEANUT SAUCE

MAKES 2 CUPS ▪ PREP TIME: 5 MINUTES ▪ COOK TIME: 5 MINUTES

DF

1½ cups unsalted chicken broth

¼ cup peanut butter

2 tablespoons rice vinegar

1 teaspoon sriracha

1 tablespoon fish sauce

1 tablespoon soy sauce

½ teaspoon grated fresh ginger

½ teaspoon sesame oil

¼ teaspoon chili oil

PER SERVING (2 tablespoons)
Calories: 32; Total carbs: 1g;
Net carbs: 1g; Fiber: 0g; Fat: 2g;
Protein: 2g; Sodium: 236mg

Peanut sauce is a delicious accompaniment to more than Thai food. It is delicious on meats and vegetables and in stir-fries. So, if you have a hankering for some Thai peanut sauce, this tasty version will surely appease your taste buds.

1 In a small saucepan over medium-high heat, stir together the chicken broth, peanut butter, rice vinegar, sriracha, fish sauce, soy sauce, ginger, sesame oil, and chili oil.

2 Heat for 3 to 5 minutes, or just to a simmer.

BLUE CHEESE DRESSING

MAKES 2¼ CUPS ▪ PREP TIME: 5 MINUTES

GF V

8 ounces crumbled blue cheese

1 cup sour cream

1 cup mayonnaise

1 tablespoon red wine vinegar

½ teaspoon garlic powder

¼ teaspoon freshly ground
  black pepper

Pinch cayenne pepper

PER SERVING (2 tablespoons)
Calories: 111; Total carbs: 4g;
Net carbs: 4g; Fiber: 0g; Fat: 10g;
Protein: 3g; Sodium: 248mg

Serve this delicious dressing on a salad, as a veggie dip, or accompanying Buffalo Chicken Wings (page 70). The strong salty, creamy flavor of this dressing is a source of cravings for many. Some versions include a little sugar, which increases the carb count. This one does not.

In a small bowl, mix together the blue cheese, sour cream, mayonnaise, red wine vinegar, garlic powder, black pepper, and cayenne pepper.

RANCH DRESSING

MAKES 2¼ CUPS ▪ PREP TIME: 5 MINUTES

GF V

1 cup sour cream

½ cup mayonnaise

½ cup heavy (whipping) cream

2 tablespoons almond milk

2 teaspoons freshly squeezed
lemon juice

1 teaspoon apple cider vinegar

¼ cup chopped fresh
Italian parsley

2 tablespoons chopped fresh dill

1 tablespoon chopped
fresh chives

1 garlic clove, minced

½ teaspoon salt

½ teaspoon freshly ground
black pepper

⅛ teaspoon cayenne pepper

Dash Tabasco sauce

PER SERVING (2 tablespoons)
Calories: 71; Total carbs: 3g;
Net carbs: 3g; Fiber: 0g; Fat: 6g;
Protein: 1g; Sodium: 143mg

Kids and adults alike will eat all their veggies when topped with this carb-friendly dressing. The creamy, cool ranch flavor is delicious on salads or as a dip for Fried Zucchini (page 64) or even Chicken Fingers (page 71). This version has a blend of herbs, including garlic and dill, and a little lemon to give it the tangy flavor that usually comes from buttermilk.

In a small bowl, whisk together the sour cream, mayonnaise, heavy cream, almond milk, lemon juice, cider vinegar, parsley, dill, chives, garlic, salt, black pepper, cayenne pepper, and Tabasco sauce until well blended.

BARBECUE SAUCE

MAKES 2 CUPS ▪ PREP TIME: 5 MINUTES ▪ COOK TIME: 15 MINUTES

GF V DF

2 tablespoons extra-virgin olive oil

¼ cup finely chopped onion

4 garlic cloves, minced

2 tablespoons tomato paste

1 (15-ounce) can tomato sauce

¼ cup white vinegar

2 tablespoons whiskey (optional)

½ teaspoon liquid smoke

½ teaspoon stevia

⅛ teaspoon cayenne pepper

1 teaspoon paprika

1 teaspoon chili powder

1 teaspoon salt

¼ teaspoon freshly ground black pepper

PER SERVING (2 tablespoons)
Calories: 31; Total carbs: 2g;
Net carbs: 1g; Fiber: 1g; Fat: 2g;
Protein: 1g; Sodium: 291mg

Barbecue sauce is often full of sugar. It can also be hard to give up. Fortunately, it's possible to make a sweet, spicy, smoky sauce that does your food justice without all the carbs. This version is thick, rich, and a little spicy. Fire up the grill!

1 In a medium saucepan over medium-high heat, heat the olive oil until it shimmers.

2 Add the onion. Cook for about 5 minutes, stirring occasionally, until soft.

3 Add the garlic. Cook for 30 to 60 seconds, stirring constantly, until fragrant.

4 Stir in the tomato paste. Cook for about 3 minutes, stirring constantly, until it begins to brown.

5 Stir in the tomato sauce, vinegar, whiskey (if using), liquid smoke, stevia, cayenne pepper, paprika, chili powder, salt, and black pepper. Reduce the heat to medium.

6 Simmer for about 5 minutes more, stirring occasionally, until the sauce thickens slightly.

COCKTAIL SAUCE

MAKES ¼ CUP ■ PREP TIME: 5 MINUTES

¼ cup low-carb ketchup

1 teaspoon freshly squeezed lemon juice

1 teaspoon horseradish

⅛ teaspoon hot sauce

PER SERVING (2 tablespoons)
Calories: 12; Total carbs: 2g;
Net carbs: 2g; Fiber: 0g; Fat: 0g;
Protein: 0g; Sodium: 220mg

It's cocktail time—cocktail sauce time, that is. Cocktail sauce is a sweet and spicy combination of ketchup, hot sauce, and horseradish. Many companies now make excellent low-carb ketchups. Check your local grocery store. The spicy and sweet nature of the cocktail sauce complements seafood like shrimp perfectly. Cheers!

In a small bowl, mix together the ketchup, lemon juice, horseradish, and hot sauce until well combined.

THE CLEAN FIFTEEN & DIRTY DOZEN

A nonprofit and environmental watchdog organization called Environmental Working Group (EWG) looks at data supplied by the US Department of Agriculture (USDA) and the Food and Drug Administration (FDA) about pesticide residues. Each year it compiles a list of the best and worst pesticide loads found in commercial crops. You can use these lists to decide which fruits and vegetables to buy organic to minimize your exposure to pesticides and which produce is considered safe enough to buy conventionally. This does not mean they are pesticide-free, though, so wash these fruits and vegetables thoroughly.

These lists change every year, so make sure you look up the most recent one before you fill your shopping cart. You'll find the most recent lists as well as a guide to pesticides in produce at EWG.org/FoodNews.

2015 DIRTY DOZEN

Apples
Celery
Cherry tomatoes
Cucumbers
Grapes
Nectarines
  (imported)
Peaches
Potatoes
Snap peas
  (imported)
Spinach
Strawberries
Sweet bell peppers

In addition to the dirty dozen, the EWG added two types of produce contaminated with highly toxic organo-phosphate insecticides:

Kale/Collard greens

Hot peppers

2015 CLEAN FIFTEEN

Asparagus
Avocados
Cabbage
Cantaloupe
  (domestic)
Cauliflower
Eggplant
Grapefruit
Kiwis

Mangoes
Onions
Papayas
Pineapples
Sweet corn
Sweet peas (frozen)
Sweet potatoes

MEASUREMENT CONVERSIONS

VOLUME EQUIVALENTS (LIQUID)

US STANDARD	US STANDARD (OUNCES)	METRIC (APPROXIMATE)
2 tablespoons	1 fl. oz.	30 mL
¼ cup	2 fl. oz.	60 mL
½ cup	4 fl. oz.	120 mL
1 cup	8 fl. oz.	240 mL
1½ cups	12 fl. oz.	355 mL
2 cups or 1 pint	16 fl. oz.	475 mL
4 cups or 1 quart	32 fl. oz.	1 L
1 gallon	128 fl. oz.	4 L

OVEN TEMPERATURES

FAHRENHEIT (F)	CELSIUS (C) (APPROXIMATE)
250°	120°
300°	150°
325°	165°
350°	180°
375°	190°
400°	200°
425°	220°
450°	230°

VOLUME EQUIVALENTS (DRY)

US STANDARD	METRIC (APPROXIMATE)
⅛ teaspoon	0.5 mL
¼ teaspoon	1 mL
½ teaspoon	2 mL
¾ teaspoon	4 mL
1 teaspoon	5 mL
1 tablespoon	15 mL
¼ cup	59 mL
⅓ cup	79 mL
½ cup	118 mL
⅔ cup	156 mL
¾ cup	177 mL
1 cup	235 mL
2 cups or 1 pint	475 mL
3 cups	700 mL
4 cups or 1 quart	1 L

WEIGHT EQUIVALENTS

US STANDARD	METRIC (APPROXIMATE)
½ ounce	15 g
1 ounce	30 g
2 ounces	60 g
4 ounces	115 g
8 ounces	225 g
12 ounces	340 g
16 ounces or 1 pound	455 g

RESOURCES

Here's a list of great companies that make low-carb products commercially.

Baking Mixes and Flours

Atkins Nutritionals, Inc.
www.atkins.com

Big Train
www.bigtrain.com

Bob's Red Mill
www.bobsredmill.com

Byrd Mill
www.byrdmill.com

Dixie USA, Inc.
host.trustab.org/dixieusainc

LC Foods
www.holdthecarbs.com

Beer

Amstel Light
www.amstellight.com

Corona Light
www.crownimportsllc.com/ourbrands
/coronalight.htm

Heineken Light
www.heineken.com/agegateway.aspx

Michelob Ultra Amber
www.michelobultra.com/our-beers/amber
-lager-beer.html?gclid=CLe619Pp9sQCFQ
YQ7Aodw34ApQ

Bread, Pasta, Pizza Crust, Tortillas, and Crackers

Dreamfields: Healthy Carb Living
www.dreamfieldsfoods.com

FiberRich
www.fiberrich.com

Flatout Bread
www.flatoutbread.com

Foods Alive
www.foodsalive.com

Great Low Carb Bread Co.
www.greatlowcarb.com

Joseph's Bakery
www.josephsbakery.com

La Tortilla Factory
www.latortillafactory.com

Mama Lupe's
www.netrition.com/mama_lupes_tortillas
_page.html

Santa Fe Tortilla Company Carb Chopper
www.santafetortilla.com

Chocolate and Candy

Atkins Nutritionals, Inc.
www.atkins.com

ChocoPerfection
store.chocoperfection.com

Hershey's: 1-Carb Chocolates
www.thehersheycompany.com/newsroom
/news-release.aspx?id=479042

Sensato
www.netrition.com/sensato_sf_choco_chips.html

Coconut Products

Coconut Secret
www.coconutsecret.com

Let's Do ... Organic
www.edwardandsons.com/ldo_info.itml

Condiments: Ketchup, Pickles, Relish, Barbecue Sauce, Dressings

Heinz Reduced-Sugar Ketchup
www.heinzketchup.com/Products/Heinz%20
Reduced%20Sugar%20Ketchup%2013oz

Mount Olive Pickles and Relishes
www.mtolivepickles.com/products/product
-styles/#

Muir Glen Organic
www.muirglen.com

Nature's Hollow
www.natureshollow.com

Walden Farms
www.waldenfarms.com

Ice Cream

Blue Bunny Sweet Freedom
www.bluebunny.com/Search/Products/q
/Sweet_Freedom

Breyer's CarbSmart
www.breyers.com/product/category/113546
/carbsmart

Jams, Syrups, and Preserves

Nature's Hollow
www.natureshollow.com

Walden Farms
www.waldenfarms.com

Meal Replacements (Protein Bars and Shakes)

Atkins Nutritionals, Inc.
www.atkins.com

Dixie USA, Inc.
host.trustab.org/dixieusainc

HealthSmart Foods
www.healthsmartfoods.com

La Nouba
www.lanouba.be/home.php

Sweeteners

Pyure Stevia
www.pyuresweet.com

Stevia in the Raw
www.intheraw.com/products/stevia-in-the-raw

Sweetleaf Sweet Drops and Powdered Stevia
www.sweetleaf.com/stevia-products

Swerve
www.swervesweetener.com/diabetes

Truvia
www.truvia.com

REFERENCES

Anton, Stephen D., Corby K. Martin, Hongmei Han, Sandra Coulon, William T. Cefalu, Paula Geiselman, and Donald A. Williamson. "Effects of Stevia, Aspartame, and Sucrose on Food Intake, Satiety, and Postprandial Glucose and Insulin Levels." *Appetite* 55, no. 1 (August 2010): 37–43. doi:10.1016/j.appet.2010.03.009.

Dryden, Jim. "Artificial Sweeteners May Do More Than Sweeten." Washington University in St. Louis. Newsroom. May 29, 2013. http://news.wustl.edu/news/Pages/25491.aspx. Original source article: Pepino M. Y., C. D. Tiemann, B. W. Patterson, B. M. Wice, S. Klein. "Sucralose Affects Glycemic and Hormonal Response to an Oral Glucose Load." *Diabetes Care*. Published online before print April 30, 2013. doi: 10.2337/dc12-2221.

Louden, Kathleen. "Refined Carbs May Trigger Food Addiction." *MedScape Medical News: Psychiatry*. July 2, 2013. www.medscape.com/viewarticle/807209.

Noda, K., K. Nakayama, and T. Oku. "Serum Glucose and Insulin Levels and Erythritol Balance after Oral Administration of Erythritol in Healthy Subjects." *European Journal of Clinical Nutrition* 48, no. 4 (April 1994): 286–292.

Picower Institute for Learning and Memory. "Decoding Sugar Addiction." *MIT News*. January 29, 2015. newsoffice.mit.edu/2015/decoding-sugar-addiction-0129.

Samaha, Frederick F., Nayyar Iqbal, Prakash Seshadri, Kathryn L. Chicano, Denise A. Daily, Joyce McGrory, Terrence Williams, Monica Williams, Edward J. Gracely, and Linda Stern. "A Low-Carbohydrate as Compared with a Low-Fat Diet in Severe Obesity." *The New England Journal of Medicine* 348 (May 2003): 2074–2081. doi:10.1056/NEJMoa022637.

Sharman, M. J., A. L. Gómez, W. J. Kraemer, J. S. Volek. "Very Low-Carbohydrate and Low-Fat Diets Affect Fasting Lipids and Postprandial Lipemia Differently in Overweight Men." *The Journal of Nutrition* 134, no. 4 (April 2004): 880–885.

Swerve Sweetener. "Swerve and Diabetes." Accessed April 15, 2015. www.swervesweetener.com/swerve-diabetes.

Yang, Qing. "Gain Weight by 'Going Diet?' Artificial Sweeteners and the Neurobiology of Sugar Cravings." Neuroscience 2010. *The Yale Journal of Biology and Medicine* 83, no. 2 (June 2010): 101–108. www.ncbi.nlm.nih.gov/pmc/articles/PMC2892765.

RECIPE INDEX

INDEX

CPSIA information can be obtained
at www.ICGtesting.com
Printed in the USA
BVOW05s0814221117
500840BV00039B/406/P